RETIREMENT: YOUR NEW BEGINNING

I consider the insight from this book a gift that all of us need...It is important to you, those you love and influence and to the world.

—**Lee Brower**, Empowered Wealth, LC

A whole new approach delivered sincerely, clearly and with true-life insights to help understand and prepare for retirement. A tool and reference to keep going back to - genuinely insightful!

—**Ike Elimsa**, Director Twelve12

RETIREMENT: YOUR NEW BEGINNING

LEVERAGING OVER

1000

CLIENTS

THROUGH THEIR RETIREMENT
FOR THE PAST 20 YEARS

SID MIRAMONTES

New York

RETIREMENT: YOUR NEW BEGINNING
LEVERAGING OVER 1000 CLIENTS
THROUGH THEIR RETIREMENT FOR THE PAST 20 YEARS

© 2017 SID MIRAMONTES

Published in New York, New York, by Morgan James Publishing. Morgan James and The Entrepreneurial Publisher are trademarks of Morgan James, LLC. www.MorganJamesPublishing.com

The Morgan James Speakers Group can bring authors to your live event. For more information or to book an event visit The Morgan James Speakers Group at www.TheMorganJamesSpeakersGroup.com.

ISBN 978-1-68350-126-8 paperback
ISBN 978-1-68350-128-2 eBook
ISBN 978-1-68350-127-5 hardcover
Library of Congress Control Number: 2016944740

Cover Design by:
Chris Treccani
www.3dogdesign.net

Shelfie

A **free** eBook edition is available with the purchase of this print book.

CLEARLY PRINT YOUR NAME ABOVE IN UPPER CASE

Instructions to claim your free eBook edition:
1. Download the Shelfie app for Android or iOS
2. Write your name in **UPPER CASE** above
3. Use the Shelfie app to submit a photo
4. Download your eBook to any device

In an effort to support local communities, raise awareness and funds, Morgan James Publishing donates a percentage of all book sales for the life of each book to Habitat for Humanity Peninsula and Greater Williamsburg.

Get involved today! Visit
www.MorganJamesBuilds.com

To my wife Ari, thank you for your love and support throughout all the time I have dedicated to this project. You inspire me to aspire to my best.

To my children Julian, Jenna, and Noah, I want you to know that with dedication and focus you can do anything.

To my team, Danielle, Isaiah, Paul, Teresa, and Victoria, thank you for all your input, research, advice, and all the hours you spent collectively on this project. Without you this project would not have come to fruition.

CONTENTS

FOREWORD

Albert Szent-György, known as the discoverer of Vitamin C, and Nobel Prize winner from the 1930's is quoted as saying "Discovery is seeing what everybody else has seen, and thinking what nobody else has thought."

In my experience, one of life's great challenges is dealing with the unknown. For many of us the concept of retirement, although aggressively sought after, falls into that category of the unknown. The literal definition of "retire" is to withdraw, to go away, to retreat. If we were to choose a word today for what life looks like when we hit the so-called retirement age, what is the likelihood we would select "retirement"?

So, what word would we end up with? "Second Half?" "Transformation?" "The Next Act"? "Metamorphosis"? "The Next Stage?" "Last Chance?" At least these names are closer to what "retirement" really

x | RETIREMENT: YOUR NEW BEGINNING

is. Retirement is mostly about transforming, or elevating or freedom or change or maybe it looks very much like what preceded it.

As you will read in the pages ahead, Sid Miramontes, as Albert Szent-György said, sees what everybody else sees yet paints a new picture of retirement. In fact, if Sid had his way, he would actually obliterate the word from our language entirely. Crafting a mindset shift that has evolved over several decades of working with over a thousand "retiring" individuals, Sid has settled on the concept of a "New Beginning".

Promoters of retirement programs and services like to paint the picture of retirement as sitting on the beach next to your loved one with a cold drink in hand wistfully pondering life's blessings or hours on end of sinking 20 foot putts or frequent checking of the temperature of the pool. Even when you have more than enough money to live that way, it doesn't take too long for most people to realize that you can only check the temperature in the pool so many times.

According to the Pew Research Center, 10,000 baby boomers turn 65 every day. Why should they "withdraw, go away, or retreat" from the very things that they have learned and the principles that allowed them to thrive in their daily lives up to that point? The "New Beginning" should be a **continuation** of a lifetime of learning, sharing and growing.

I have often said that the enemy of thriving is arriving. When we take on the attitude of "arriving", we surrender our growth, productivity and meaningfulness along with the opportunity to joyfully thrive. The New Beginning Mindset embraces lifelong learning, productivity and purposefulness. A thriving "New Beginning" can be and should be a time for amazing engagement, growth, connections, contributions and increased possibilities.

I congratulate you, the reader, for making the effort to be prepared. Retirement: Your New Beginning is a must read for anyone who endeavors to live in retirement and not be retired. Whether you are already retired, approaching retirement or retirement seems far away, the pages that follow will help prepare you for your personal New Beginning.

Right now three quarters of American workers believe they'll continue working past their retirement age. For some, they will keep working because they have to financially. And, as Arianna Huffington says, "Others will keep working because the "gold" in our so-called "golden years" doesn't have to come from watching sunsets."

People are living longer. Today's 70 is yesterdays 50. Most people want the same meaningfulness and purpose in this New Beginning as they had in their working years- and in many cases, they desire even more meaning and purpose.

I consider the insight from this book a gift that all of us need. I commend it to you. It is important to you, those you love and influence and to the world. Retirement: The New Beginning is like a nutrition and exercise book. It will give you great insight, a new mindset and new questions to ask. But, you can't benefit from just reading it. You have to do it. You have to eat it. It is nutritious.

Lee M. Brower
Founder
Empowered Wealth, LC*

Empowered Wealth is a global leader in optimizing Gratitude, Leadership and "True Wealth. "Everything** that Empowered Wealth does, they believe in empowering leaders, families and organizations.*

NOTE TO READER

Helping someone plan for retirement is a very personal process. One of the cornerstones of my business has always been to educate the client— something we take very seriously at Miramontes Capital. Maybe because of this I've often had clients suggest that I write a book. The idea of putting together a book of commonly shared information was simple enough, but I wanted it to be more than just financial advice.

Over the years, I have met a lot of clients. Some situations are similar for each person, but others are totally unique to each individual—the personal, the exceptional, the human side of retirement. It's this part that finally made me decide to write this book.

By far the greatest thing about working in retirement is the people. It never ceases to amaze me how committed, diligent, and good my clients have been, and I'm happy to get the pleasure of assisting them in reaching their financial goals. More than this, though, I get to learn from them. Every single client I've met has followed their dream for retirement in their own way, and by doing so has shown me just a little bit more of what motivates people when they plan for their retirement.

I dedicate this book to all the individuals that I've met over the years—from those early mechanics to the CEO I had lunch with today—they have all helped me grow. I write this book in honor of everyone who I've seen achieve their dreams. This book is a thank you to my clients for inspiring me and helping me achieve mine.

Sid Miramontes

PART I
ADJUSTING TO RETIREMENT

THE RIGHT CHOICE

Is your future brighter than your past? Imagine what it's going to be like not to have to work anymore. Do you envision your retirement as a time that will surpass your working years in fulfillment and meaning?

Have you ever given up something you liked for something you loved? Think of when you were young, and you first experienced the feeling of saving up for something special. Do you think the feeling of finally retiring will resemble this?

Will all the wisdom you've gained over the years of your life be used for your benefit moving forward? Each of us continually learns as we go through our lives, whether we realize it or not. What experiences have you had that will shape you in the years to come?

These questions and many more are what we use to gain insight and understanding into who you really are and what your future will hold, to help you make the right choices for retirement. Maybe you see vacations, travel, relaxing on a beach in Spain, or driving across the country. Maybe you envision volunteering for an organization you love, or enjoying the freedom of consulting in a way you were never able to before. You might see yourself relaxing and spending time with your grandchildren, or helping out family or loved ones.

There are thousands of different ways you can add meaning to your life. But for anyone in any walk of life, the transition that we face in retirement can really shake things up. As your life changes, it takes time to recalibrate, to find your values again. You might also find that retirement is the time when you stretch out and find your potential.

It's exciting to plan for things like this. However, your goals aren't going to achieve themselves. And the intimidating thing is that you are responsible *right now* for making sure you'll be able to achieve your goals. Every single person retires. But the way people plan for this stage of life is personal and different. For some people, it can feel like there is a canyon between who they are and who they want to be when they retire. As their retirement approaches, they realize they need help.

It is my purpose to provide meaningful steps toward finding a path to retirement. Moreover, I want to make retirement and retirement planning a more meaningful process. No matter where you are in the timeline—whether already retired or in the process of retiring—I want this book to provide you with encouragement and direction. More than anything, I hope you're left with a sense of community. Even if our portfolios are completely different, it's important to find common ground in the challenges that retirees face. We all have choices to make. After reading what I've written here, my hope is that you'll be that much closer to making the right choices for your retirement.

USING THE
RIGHT CHOICE QUESTIONS

For your convenience, you'll find all The Right Choice questions collected in the appendix at the back of this book, as well as on our website at miramontescapital.com.

Planning for your retirement is a personal process, and it's my goal to help you position yourself within the information and advice contained within this book. In order to help you engage with the text more, I've included a discussion or journal question at the end of each section. These are designed to help you personalize the information, as well as give you the chance to take steps toward preparing and planning. These questions can stand as discussion starters for you and your partner, and can be a wonderful way to warm you both up towards a difficult subject, as retirement often can be. In addition, you can work through the topics yourself, preferably responding to the prompts by writing in a journal. The nature of retirement and retirement planning makes it interesting and useful to look back on the ways you've changed throughout the process.

RETIREMENT IS
THE NEW BEGINNING

As I've continued to progress in my career, resulting in my decision in 2015 to move from the wire house I worked for and become an independent RIA, or Registered Investment Adviser, I've kept my eyes open. The journey has taught me a lot about people, what most of us feel when confronted with the challenge of retirement, and most importantly, some universal needs in the area of financial advice.

I've met with thousands of people from all walks of life over the last twenty years, and I've come to realize that the one thing true for all people, despite how their retirement situations vary, is that retirement is a new beginning—it's *the* new beginning—for each individual's life. When you retire, you're faced with a possibility for renewal and reinvention that is basically unequaled in any other transition in your life. It's up to you to decide what your goals are and how you're going to achieve them.

Meet People Where They Are

One of the best lessons I ever learned about this business was to meet people where they are. The first group of people I advised at the beginning of my financial career were bus drivers and mechanics. I would literally meet them where they were, stooping down to where a mechanic was doing repairs under a bus to talk about savings habits. More than once I assembled the drivers and mechanics together into the rowed seats of the very machines they operated and worked on to give them an overview of the difference between bonds and stocks.

These folks were workers. They were genuine and down to earth. Many had never thought seriously about the concept of retirement, and it was obvious that these folks needed information. In my initial meetings with these clients, I began by spewing all the information I could, weighted heavily with every industry-specific term I could muster. I must have sounded very "professional" – but they didn't get a thing from it. I think for my first few clients I only succeeded in scaring the stuffing out of them.

> *"In retirement planning, every single person has different needs."*

Luckily, the story didn't end there. Time and experience taught me that financial planning is about simplifying. I realize now that I was denying those early clients and myself the honesty of interacting with them on a personal level. The maxim I have now built my business upon is that in retirement planning, every single person has different needs, and requires a plan that reflects those specific needs.

Retirement: It's 50% Psychological, 50% Financial

When you retire, you go through two big transitions. One is financial—preparing yourself to live beyond receiving a paycheck. The other equally important transition is a psychological one. Retirement is a new beginning, and that means closing the book on one chapter in order to begin the next. The psychological transition is learning how to fully process that. If you're going to have a successful retirement, you have to plan for both of these transitions.

A couple of years ago, I helped a couple retire. They both, and especially the wife, were really hesitant. She was worried they wouldn't be able to maintain their lifestyle. But she also feared the different lifestyle that comes with retirement and of having to redefine one's self. We met a number of times over the year to educate them and help pinpoint what was most important to help them construct their most meaningful life. Slowly but surely, as my client's wife came to better understand the process of retiring, a transformation happened. She found that she no longer feared the idea of redefining herself after work. This transformation was possible because we were able to simplify their retirement. They could grasp the plan and take ownership of it, and were therefore freed up to move forward in the retirement process. Based on the needs of their lifestyle, the couple decided that she would retire first at the age of 60. With her husband working for a few years more, she was able to delay her social security until the age of 66. Their situation wasn't an exceptional or tricky one. They simply needed to be met where they were.

As of now, they take regular long trips across the country. We recently received a beautiful picture of them, sent from the road, showing them in their new motor home overlooking a lush, green valley in Tennessee. Theirs is a success story, and it shows just how related the financial and the psychological pieces of planning are. When you're comfortable about your financial decisions, your life decisions come together more easily.

The Right Information Makes A Difference

Another client story shows how just a little information, when applied to a specific situation, can make all the difference. I met with a couple who were really discouraged about their present retirement situation. They had amassed $60,000 in debt and were having difficulty making the $2,600 monthly payments while working. They assumed that if they couldn't pay down the debt while receiving a salary, there was no way it would be eliminated in retirement. They were scared that the debt would fall to their heirs, which they could not abide.

We looked at their options and found that their IRA would support a one-time distribution that would eliminate the debt. I advised them that knocking out the debt this way would save thousands in interest over their retirement, in addition to saving them from the monthly payments their budget couldn't support. Suddenly, retirement seemed possible again.

Eliminating that stress opened doors for the couple that were unimaginable before. After retirement, they took advantage of their new freedom by traveling to places they had always wanted to see. Spending time with their grandchildren, they say, has really added a new dimension of happiness to their life. They both received a scare a few years back when the husband had to undergo a quadruple bypass surgery, and that has made them both perfectly aware of how important it is to enjoy their quality of life while they can.

When you're unfamiliar with investments and retirement accounts—which most people are – such basic information can be the difference between a happy retirement and a stressful one. How much more true is this when it comes to the more esoteric points about retirement, like tax advantages, which can save thousands of dollars? The happiness I can give people, like in the case above, makes me love being a financial architect.

Our Dedication to Education Goes Both Ways

When asked to describe my method for giving retirement advice, I arrived at two main principles: first-class communication, and a dedication to education. It's my goal to educate clients in any areas they lack, whether that be the Social Security system, assisting them with their company's benefits package, or helping them to get the most out of their stock options. Moreover, we promote continuing education any way we can. We customize market updates, we hold client breakfasts to stay in touch, we host quarterly events where we cover market updates as well as other areas that may affect retirement, such as health and nutrition. The more educated you are, the better the decisions we are able to make together.

This is as true for us as it is for our clients. A guiding principle behind the services we offer at Miramontes Capital is allowing our clients to educate us about their life.

My client Dave had a lot of stress on his shoulders. Not only did he provide for his spouse and all of his children, his ailing mother also counted on him for support. Dave's mother had provided for him throughout his upbringing, despite the challenges she faced as a single mother in a foreign country. Dave felt that it was his responsibility to repay her for all that she had done for him, and so it was imperative for us design his plan with this in mind.

We educated him on the process of retiring and customizing a program that would support his entire family and put him at ease. Finally, the day of his retirement came. Soon after, Dave told me he had finally realized there was more to life than the confines of his office. When he was working, he was in "providing mode." The love he showed his family was monetary. After retiring he was able to show his love through spending time with his family. He was able to share his life and his experiences with them, and that's what has made his retirement meaningful.

When we start working with a client, we want to know their fears, their hopes, their habits, and what they want out of retirement. In the process, we find that our clients learn a great deal about themselves, too. We usually don't choose to think about these crucial issues, about what matters to us and what doesn't, and in retirement that becomes everything. That's why it's just as important to offer support, in addition to advice. Our practical, personal approach enables our clients to educate us about what their most meaningful life looks like. After this, all they have to do is allow us to help them make it a reality.

The Right Choice

I hope this section helped you realize that the process of reviewing your finances with a professional is a personal and intimate one.

- What are some of the attributes you want your retirement planner to have?
- Go to miramontescapital.com and take a moment to look over the "Roadmap to Retirement" resource available on the website.

THE APARTMENT BUILDING
YOU OWN IS ON FIRE

"Retirement isn't scary, the process is. Let us simplify it for you."
—Sid

Imagine that, after a life's worth of hard work, you've saved enough to make the huge investment of buying an apartment building. You sign the paperwork, you hand over ALL your retirement savings—your pension and your 401(k), and the building is yours. Now, your livelihood and life's work is tied up in this one venture. You decide to hire a property manager to take care of the establishment. With this person holding the reins of your life, how often are you going to want to check up on your investment? How often are you going to visit the building?

"We're going to be there every day!" most people say, "Every month at the least!" It's a natural response. Who among us could comfortably say, "Sure, I trust my manager—I'll just come once a year to check if everything's all right"? And yet, this is precisely what the vast majority of investment professionals ask you to do. After you meet initially to set up your portfolio, they'll schedule you for an annual checkup—just one meeting a year for one of the most important aspects of your life.

Let's go back to your apartment building. It's one year later and you're meeting with your manager. He's going to tell you, "OK, termites have eaten into the walls on the first floor. We need to take care of it. The tenants have painted the building purple for some reason. Let's take care of it. The west section of the building has burned down because of an electrical fire. Let's talk about our plan to rebuild it." Over a year, *anything* could happen to your investments, and these changes, good or bad, can potentially alter your needs and plans in substantial ways. We live in an ever-fluctuating world. The markets change, but the needs of the client and their lifestyle choices change too. That's why you need a proactive plan when you retire, not a reactive plan, which has become the industry standard. To achieve this, I developed the "Miramontes Method," outlined below, which includes constant and continuous communication.

Over the course of this book I'll outline what a good financial architect does, along with practical knowledge every retiree needs to know. At Miramontes Capital, we design our clients' portfolios by the same principal that governs an amazing work of art: perfect attentiveness to a clearly stated goal yields beautiful results. Defining a goal is your first and most important step as the retiree. Then it's our job, as your financial architects, to design a retirement plan that helps you achieve that goal. Unlike paintings, though, which are painted once and are finished, a successful retirement demands

"Perfect attentiveness to a clearly stated goal yields beautiful results."

continual vigilance to make sure that it still resembles the portfolio you set out to make.

Constant Communications and Analysis:
The Miramontes Method

When it comes to your "apartment building," Miramontes Capital has a method in place.

Here's an overview:

1. We review your lifestyle. A lot goes into our introductory meetings with clients. Later, as you enter retirement, we'll be communicating with you every 30-45 days to ensure your lifestyle is represented in your plan.

2. We communicate. Your portfolio is at the center. Every 30-45 days, we analyze your needs and your expectations for retirement and actively communicate the best options available to you. It's this active and preemptive method that ensures your investment is taken care of.

3. We adjust. As your spending habits, market information, and other factors change, we make sure that your portfolio reflects these changes. Nothing is more important to ensure the stability of your "apartment building."

ADJUSTING YOUR MINDSET

"Self-reverence, self-knowledge, self-control — These three alone lead life to sovereign power."
—Alfred Lord Tennyson

When you take a look at your daily life, what do you see? Most people get up, take a shower, eat some kind of breakfast and get ready to go to work. They get to work and get started, maybe answering emails, making some phone calls, going to meetings. Around noon, they take their short lunch, spend the afternoon wrapping up work and get ready to go back home. They commute back, eat dinner with their family, watch TV or maybe read a book to unwind. Then they'll go to sleep at around 10pm, wake up, do the same thing four more times, then it's the weekend. On Saturday they may get up late, spend some time with their family. On Sunday they watch sports, go to church, get ready for Monday, and that's their week. They'll do this fifty-one more times and then the year is over. They'll do that about thirty-five more times and they're retired— it's time for their New Beginning.

When we omit the personal aspects of our life, as I did above, we find it hard to tell one person from another. Luckily, that's not all there is. Each of our lives is meaningful for the color we add to it. Far from being just extra information, these things have a serious bearing on the success of our retirement. For most of us, our accounts are just the safety net to make sure that nothing gets in the way of achieving what we want – which is different for everyone.

> *"For most of us, it isn't just about money for money's sake. First and foremost, we're after our most meaningful lives."*

This section of the book[1] is dedicated to what I think is most crucial for retirees, and most often neglected by retirement professionals: the personal side. That's why the first few meetings with a new client are best used working with the client to help them understand that their mindset may need to change. The next few chapters outline a few common concepts that, when understood, can help you think of your retirement in a healthy way.

Time and Budgeting: More is Less

If I were to ask most retirees what the biggest change will be after they retire, a lot would say the added free time they'll have. With all this added free time, will your expenses go up, go down, or stay about the same? Let's take a small example: during your working years, you frequented Starbucks on the weekends with your wife, getting a pastry and a cup

---

1   Most, but not all of the personal facts throughout this book came directly from my clients; I've changed details to keep their anonymity intact, as well as to fit my purposes.

of coffee each. If you had time, maybe you'd get a refill, spending about 15 dollars for a relaxing Saturday morning—a simple indulgence you couldn't work into your weekdays.

How do you think your coffee budget is going to change now that you have reached the weekend of your life? How will your habits change now that you've got a good chunk more of time and a subscription to *The Economist* to read through? If you're like some of my clients, you might find that the expenses you don't have to worry about anymore have seamlessly been replaced by expenses that were never there before.

Every single person's spending habits are as different and complex as their life. Likewise, every person's spending habits change after retirement in surprising, personal ways. I have arrived at an axiom from the stories I hear every day: when one expense goes out the front door, another comes in the window. What I've realized from being in the business for over 20 years is that more time will eat away more

> *"A common pattern for budgeting is that when one expense goes out the front door, another comes in the window."*

money. My point is that the 85% myth is just that—an overly optimistic myth that I've seen disproven time and time again. Plan for 100%. Plan for 110-125%. It's a good idea to have your plans factor in all possibilities.

Retirement: Three and a Half Times Your Life

> *"No man is fit to command another that cannot command himself."*
> **—William Penn**

There is one huge distinction I want to make, and this is where I feel a lot of soon-to-be retirees have emotional uncertainty: retirement means retirement from work, not from life. *End of Work Syndrome,* where retirees feel a little lost as they adjust to their new routine, is easy to fall into in the lead-up to retirement, and it's felt most acutely in the first 6 months after retirement begins. New retirees can be fearful of the future. It may be fear of deteriorating health, or a fear of feeling useless. Both of these feelings can be traced back to one thing: a fear of time - running out of time, or having too much time and nothing to do with it.

The truth is, in no way does having more time translate to less usefulness. The key to any gift is using it, and it's crucial for the retiree to plan to make sure they are not going to waste the amazing gift of their retirement. Retirement is not the end of your life. If anything, it's your life magnified. When you were working, if you were lucky, the weekend meant you had two days of free time to plan and enjoy. Compare this to a person who has retired, who has seven full days of free time. The difference is five days: a 350% increase in time.

% Increase of Free Time After Retirement

Before Retirement	During Retirement	Percent Increase
2 Days of free time	7 Days of free time	350% more!

What a gift.

The claim I'm making here is not an emotional one—it's a mathematical one. Use that 350% more time to enrich your life through pursuing what matters, whatever makes you feel fulfilled. The key, the prerequisite for all this meaningful self-discovery, is a *plan*. You can't get what you want without a roadmap to get there.

So what is your "New Beginning" going to look like? How are you going to utilize your most meaningful life?

The Right Choice

A) Imagine you woke up in a world where all your loved ones were safe and provided for, you had no responsibilities, and you could use your time to do anything. What would you do? Write or sketch your perfect, worry-free life.

B) Successfully managing your time is one of the greatest keys to a successful retirement. Think about your life now. In what ways are you a good time manager, and in what ways can you use a little work? Do your answers help you perceive potential problems you may have once you're retired?

RETIREMENT FEARS

It is impossible to know how the new phase of retirement is going to feel and how deeply it will affect you—until it happens. I want share some of the common fears people have about the process of retiring, so we can prepare for them both financially and psychologically.

What About My Lifestyle?

Fear is a powerful motivator, and the fear of losing money is a substantial one. But overwhelmingly, the greatest fear people have about retirement is not losing their money, but rather losing their lifestyle. Many soon-to-be retirees are uncertain about just *how* different things will be. Many different fears about retirement fall under this umbrella, including:

- I don't want to live less comfortably.
- I don't want to go back to work.
- I don't want to lose connections with my friends.

- I want to stay active.
- I don't want to settle for lower-quality health insurance.

Nearly every aspect of the planning process relates back to knowing the financial details of your life—in other words, having a monthly budget. Through this important document, you'll be able to see what "normal" is for your family, and so be able to better understand how much difference retirement will make. Moreover, on the psychological level, simply reviewing your monthly budget can better prepare your mind for the transition.

Most of the time, the financial aspects of retirement planning begin to fall into place first. For your plan to be successful, though, it really can't stop there. Let's look at some points that deal more specifically with that other, more human side of preparing for retirement: your life!

How Do I Say It?

Many clients told me how hard it was to discuss the fact that they wanted to retire with their spouses. The subject of leaving work is intimidating because of the possible feelings of fear and uncertainty for the future it may bring up in your spouse. Moreover, telling one's spouse can be more difficult for some. You can imagine how hard it would be to say, "Honey, I'm thinking of retiring" if you've *never* talked about it before. As such, my best piece of advice for couples is to make sure that when you bring up retirement, it isn't a foreign topic!

What to Say

As is true with most difficult things in life, we want to minimize emotions and maximize productive discussion. Having a plan is a good way to achieve this. With a structure in place, you'll find it easier to speak from the heart about this huge transition. Tell your partner how you're feeling, physically and emotionally. Relate your intentions with as much detail as possible. Try to give a timeline that shows the planning and thought you've put into it. Finally, try your best to express why you think this is the best plan, and if necessary, assure him or her that it's going to be OK. Sincerity and forethought go a long way.

Saying Goodbye to Work

When you finally say goodbye to your workplace, you'll likely be confronted with a wide range of feelings. After spending the main portion of your life in the work force—some largely with the same company— you'll have grown attached to the people, the place, and even the work schedule. As such, it can be very hard to let go. There's no easy or "normal" way to confront these complex feelings. Stay close with the ones you love during the transition, and try to keep in tune with what you're feeling, however you've been accustomed to doing that, whether through journaling, prayer, meditation, or just talking with your spouse and loved ones.

As the transition unfolds, you're likely to see a significant reduction in things to do. You're also going to realize that the time you have is precious and you'll want to make the most of it. So schedule your time in a way that satisfies you. You can visit your children more often, use the time to make some home improvements, volunteer, or find a hobby that matches your interests. Just as you need to plan how our finances will progress, it's very important to take the time to plan how you'll use your free time. By doing so you can avoid the potential stress and depression that may come from transitioning away from your old lifestyle.

What to Do

The longer you wait to start thinking and planning for your retirement, the more likely you will be to have fears about it. We've designed our business model to never neglect the human concerns that retirees have. We do things like take care of the burden of paperwork, giving you the freedom to think about the more important issues at hand. Dale Carnegie summed it up nicely when he said, "Inaction breeds doubt and fear. Action breeds confidence and courage. If you want to conquer fear, do not sit at home and think about it. Go out and get busy." For your psychological, as well as your financial well-being, go out there and get busy.

The Right Choice

Create a detailed budget, including all your income and expenses. Now go through your budget (preferably with your partner) and try to note what will change about it after retirement. Which expenses will increase? Which will likely go down?

RETIREMENT WITH
YOUR PARTNER

When many of my clients look back on their life from retirement, it's not surprising that the one constant throughout all of the changes was their spouse. Upon retirement, it's likely that apart from friends and acquaintances, most find themselves largely with their husband or wife. You and your spouse are partners in this life together—emotionally, physically, and financially. Each couple's partnership is different. I've learned that even more than individuals, every couple has different views, needs, experiences, and fears.

I also often see something that makes me believe that the overwhelming amount of technology we have at our fingertips has distracted us from communicating with our partner. It is a common scenario: A couple will come in for their first scheduled appointment with me. The discussion will go well as we discuss more of the general questions, like what they hope to get out of retirement, what they've done so far to prepare, and plenty about their personal life. Then, inevitably, a topic comes up that can put a damper on the mood if they aren't prepared: their debt.

Almost anything can happen when the question comes up. Each spouse has their own credit card. Neither spouse knows the other's balance. Spouse one simply assumes spouse two is responsibly paying off the credit card, but it turns out that he or she was only paying the minimum balance. Spouse two doesn't even know about that high-interest credit card the other received through a retailer. This type of interaction happens at every income bracket. I can't tell you how many times I've seen a partner's face color at the mention of the amount of debt the couple is responsible for. I've even had spouses call me separately and ask me very earnestly not to mention this or that debt he or she has been hiding.

In a general sense these uncomfortable meetings for clients are all a result of one thing: lack of communication. Here then, is my first and most important bit of advice for couples as they prepare to retire: start talking about your finances with each other *now*—no matter what age you are. It's my goal to minimize the shock of the transition into retirement; it should be your goal not to aggravate that stress by holding on to those extra surprises for your spouse.

There are a wealth of free financial planning resources, some listed in the appendix at the end of this book, that can make this process much less painful for you and your spouse. This is an invaluable step if you're preparing to meet with us, as it allows us to really get down to your finances without worrying what one or the other partner is thinking.

Preparing for Your Partner

One of the most common fears that spouses express to me is that they don't want their loved ones to be left in need. Due to the difference in male and female life expectancy, the odds are that most husbands are going to have to make preparations for their wives after they're gone. This means ensuring your spouse is the designated beneficiary on all accounts and assets such as 401(k)s and IRAs. Luckily, spouses are usually the default beneficiaries of such assets.

One big complication of such matters is if you were previously married. Divorce can seriously complicate matters of inheritance, so as a rule, you want to be proactive and crystal-clear when it comes to such legal matters—you can't simply rely on the divorce decree. One of my clients, Ernie, was retiring from a major firm. He assumed that his ex-spouse would get her own pension, but later on, found out that this was not the case. As we checked the divorce decree, we found that she was entitled to receive half of his pension for the time that they were married and had already taken that portion years ago. After this discovery, we had to make significant adjustments to his portfolio, debt planning, and social security. Because of this major hit on his pension, he had to delay his retirement plans. Through some diligence and financial planning, we were able to turn the situation around, but it goes to show why doing research beforehand and having a living trust set up is crucial, so you are aware of anything that may affect your finances before you retire.

This is why setting up a trust and meeting with a trust attorney becomes an important piece of your financial planning. It may be an awkward topic to bring up, but it's a crucial question when you and your spouse are reviewing your finances.

It may be, too, that you and your spouse don't want part of your retirement assets to go to the other – for example, if your assets are such that he or she doesn't need them and someone else does. In any case, just remember to get everything in writing as soon as possible. States have different legal requirements for questions of this nature. Just do your homework or see a financial professional who can answer the questions for you.

Spouses Feel That Everything Is Their Responsibility

Retirement planning, especially if you're married, needs to be a joint effort – even if one of you is used to being the one who takes care of financial matters. This may take some careful adjustments in mindset. Communicating about financial decisions may not be second nature. Cultivating a regular communication schedule and including your spouse in big decisions can really bring you together as you enter retirement.

Respect Each Other's Space

An interesting situation that a lot of married couples don't really anticipate has to do with personal space. The wife of one client, Ike, had been a homemaker, and had regularly been home by herself for twenty years before Ike retired. As all humans do, the wife had a scheduled routine: she did bills in the morning at the kitchen table; she did the laundry at a certain time on a certain day; she took two hours most afternoons to do some work from the home office; then she enjoyed her valuable quiet time to read at a specific time and place.

You can imagine the awkwardness Ike and his wife went through as they transitioned into retirement. This dynamic is not an uncommon one. For those of us not in this situation, it's easy to chuckle at the idea. But for the couple weathering the transition into retirement, the added tension is real. As a new retiree, what could be worse than sensing from your spouse that you don't belong in your own home?

It takes a retiree about three months to start getting the hang of the new rhythm of life, and about six months to figure out how retirement works for both spouses. Simple methods you can use to prepare include, first of all, learning what your partner's schedule will be. Talk about which times of the day each of you will be around the house, which times you'll need space, and plan accordingly. It all comes back to clear and defined communication. Something as simple as a shared dry erase calendar can add convenience and clarity to your scheduling. Hang it in a common area like the kitchen, where it's easy to add to and check.

The Right Choice

Discuss your daily schedule with your spouse. What about the schedule will remain the same after retirement and what will change? If you're actually nearing retirement, buy a dry erase board and map out both of your schedules.

RETIREMENT: IT WILL HAPPEN TO YOU (AND IT MAY SURPRISE YOU)

I had met with Mike for about three years. He was a senior manager at a major utility firm, and had spent thirty years giving himself to his job. He was flexible and responsible, and there weren't any significant adjustments required to get him on the right path to retirement.

Then one day, something changed. Mike started looking closely at the way he was using his time. He wanted to spend more time with his family while he still felt young. So we sat down together and decided that his current economic situation provided him with a strategy to retire earlier than originally planned. It took a lot of cooperation—we included his wife in a number of the meetings as well. There was a lot to do, but within just a few months, he was retired.

Mike chose to believe that his future could be brighter than his past. He had always defined himself by his high-level position in his company.

But almost immediately after retirement, Mike's priorities shifted, and he was able to find success in a totally different way.

Mike had always liked to surf. Even with the demanding schedule of an executive, he made a point to occasionally take time for it in the mornings before work. Naturally, one of his first thoughts when he realized he was going to retire was that he would surf more. Then, shortly after retiring, Mike was struck with a big thought: how lucky he was to have his health. What a blessing to be able to surf every day, if he wanted to. Mike thought of others who weren't as lucky, people who had suffered injuries and would never be able to experience the feeling of being out in the water, feeling the movements of the ocean. Then, he got an idea.

I learned of Mike's newfound success at one of our client breakfasts that we regularly organize. He told me he had organized a community service event in which he meets with wounded war veterans and gives them surfing lessons. It is a great source of pride for him that his family supports this new passion to help others. It's become an amazing time of bonding for the whole family, and a chance to learn from his new friends.

Mike couldn't be more pleased. He said he had no idea retirement could feel so good. Not only is he doing what he's always loved, he's also helping others do things they didn't think were possible, and as an added bonus, he gets to be surrounded by the people he loves most. It doesn't get more meaningful than that.

A Flick of the Switch

Like Mike, some people who have started their retirement planning many years in advance don't necessarily adhere strictly to the date they determine for their retirement to begin. The reason behind this can be found in one of the deep governing principles of life: there is only so much in our own lives that we are actually in control of. It may sometimes feel like we are swimming in choices. However, when you zoom out from the little decisions, so much happens to us that we are not responsible for and sometimes not even aware of.

A majority of people will find that their retirement plan and their actual retirement can't be compared. People plan to retire when they aren't yet ready to retire; when they *do* become ready to retire, the change happens instantaneously—like the flick of a switch.

This change may be brought about by any number of factors. The first undeniable factor is your health—if your job is one that requires physical exertion, the odds are that one day your body will simply say, "Hey! That's about all I've got!" The second factor is your mind. Often, individuals begin to feel that working any further will cause too many complications for them, their coworkers, or family, and so they realize that it's time to retire. Perhaps an unforeseen shake-up at the work place makes it either advantageous or necessary to retire. Our personal lives, too, are full of people, places, and things that just won't fit into our set plan.

Luckily for my client Mike, he started planning with us early on, and because of this, he had the ability to adjust his plan when he felt it was time to retire. We grow into our retirement plan, and sometimes adjustments are needed as our life and perspectives change. Much like installment payments help us afford a large purchase, a consistent planning process distributes the transition of retirement over a longer period of time, making it more manageable. But there's a distinction that needs to be made in the planning process, which we'll see in another client story: the distinction between planning *to retire* and planning *for retirement.*

Reconsidering Retirement: What to Do Early On

I had a client named Mila who was caught off-guard by the abrupt closing of her division at work, which meant an unexpected early retirement. When the dust settled on the transition, her biggest concern was the feeling of "not knowing what to do or how to do it," in her words. At our meeting, I gave her some resources to look into.

Thirty days later I checked in to see how she was doing. She explained to me that she was already enrolled in a photography class *and* had hired a personal trainer. Fast forward a few years and Mila had a schedule so full of photography, training, biking, and family that she told me she didn't have much time for anything else.

Retirement, for most people, comes in stages. For most of my clients, the first three to eight weeks feel like a vacation they've been looking forward to for decades. This "honeymoon" stage soon fades and they are overcome by concerns for how their time will be dedicated. What you can do now, long before retirement, is to assess what is important to you in specific, measurable and goal-oriented ways. I'd recommend creating a list informed by the general categories of life:

"Much like installment payments help us afford a large purchase, a consistent planning process distributes the transition of retirement over a longer period of time, making it more manageable."

- Health
- Family
- Friends
- Spirituality
- Philanthropy
- Personal Development

And so on, as you see appropriate. From these categories, start making more specific goals. Make short-term and long-term goals, and hold yourself accountable. You can track your progress, looking back over time to see how you've grown. If you put in the extra effort at the beginning, and then a little more effort every day to maintain your direction, you'll be happy with the results.

The Right Choice

Great transitions such as retirement take preparation on a number of levels. Check our website at miramontescapital.com for a list of resources to make sure your retirement gets off to a healthy start.

PART II
BREAKING IT DOWN

FINANCIAL ADVISOR VS. FINANCIAL ARCHITECT

"Different isn't always better, but better is always different."
—Lee Brower

I've never taken very well to the term "advisor." Something about the word sounds detached, legalistic, and not personal. We consider ourselves ***architects of your new beginning***, which means your portfolio and your retirement plan are constructed depending on your choices and preferences. The process of planning and designing your portfolio should be as creative as planning and designing a great building, and that's what we're here to do for you.

The Right Choice

Think about your ideal investment professional. Do you feel you can ask this person anything? Can you see yourself with this person long-term? Will the services you receive include ongoing education? Is the professional's team supportive and open to you?

These crucial questions should inform any decision you make regarding your investment professional.

"We're architects: the process of planning and designing your portfolio should be as creative as planning and designing a great building."

FIDUCIARY RESPONSIBILITY MAKES THE DIFFERENCE

After saving for retirement for most of your working life, choosing the person to manage those funds is a huge exercise in trust. Unfortunately, having a knowledgeable professional who is willing to communicate with you may not be enough to ensure that that professional is acting in your best interests. If the person you're relying on to manage your retirement funds is not designated as a fiduciary, you and your funds may be subjected to undue risk or fees.

The Responsibility of a Fiduciary
- A fiduciary has certain responsibilities that he or she must uphold:
- Fiduciaries act solely in the interest of the clients whose funds they are responsible for, with the exclusive purpose of providing benefits to them.

- They are responsible for carrying out their duties prudently.
- Fiduciaries have a duty to care for their clients, meaning they must show due diligence in following up to ensure that the plan they construct is still in the client's best interests.
- They are also responsible for being transparent about fees involved in the investments recommended by the fiduciary.

There are state and federal statutes which define fiduciary responsibility. Among the governing bodies responsible for enforcing a person or entity's fiduciary responsibility is ERISA, or Employee Retirement Investment Security Act. Fiduciaries who do not follow principles of conduct mentioned above may be personally liable to restore any losses, making it in their own interest as well to ensure that they keep their client's best interests first[1].

Miramontes Capital and Fiduciary Responsibility

In the ever-shifting regulatory climate, my team and I are proud to take the fiduciary guidelines mentioned here not as a requirement we have to scramble to hold ourselves to, but as a confirmation of what I've always believed is required in the relationship between our team of retirement architects and the clients we serve. At Miramontes Capital, we take the trust that our clients have placed in us very seriously. We work to take fiduciary responsibility and make it personal.

The Right Choice

Your Goals and Responsibility

After considering the trust that goes into partnering with a financial professional, how do you expect your fiduciary to help you to shape and achieve your goals for retirement? For more information on how Miramontes Capital cares for your finances and your future, visit miramontescapital.com.

YOUR COMFORT ZONE

A number of years ago I had a prospective client, Kay, ask me if I was more aggressive or conservative in my advice – a question I'm often asked. I politely turned it around to her, and asked, "Are you aggressive or conservative?" Kay had never really invested before, was very shrewd about saving, and didn't commonly withdraw from the account. I told her that if she wanted to continue on the retirement path she began a long time ago, we would present her with a relatively conservative plan.

There is no standard retirement formula that works for everyone. If a financial professional has a set answer for the question of whether they are aggressive or conservative, walk out of their office. The answer must be relative and personal. If you've never invested a dime in your life, even investing in McDonald's, Microsoft, or Apple are more aggressive moves in comparison to just putting your money in your bank account.

With knowledge comes confidence, and as such, I sometimes tell clients that retirement is a time where a little branching out, both socially and financially, may be a good thing.[2] On the other hand, when we're conservative, we're comforted by what we know and what we understand.

It's a question that bears thinking about during the planning process, and I'd recommend not letting an investment professional make the decision for you. If you're trying to figure out whether your financial situation calls for a more conservative or a more aggressive approach, you can consider questions such as whether or not you'll have other income sources during retirement, or whether you're interested in leaving an amount of capital behind to loved ones.

"If a financial professional has a set answer for the question of whether they are aggressive or conservative, walk out of their office."

Once you have thought about your situation for yourself, you'll less likely be persuaded to accept something that isn't for you when given financial advice. But more importantly, you'll be conscious of choosing someone who is willing to take a personal approach to your finances, who thinks of you as a person, and is willing to learn about your unique situation.

---

2   This is a generalization I by no means intend to be taken as specific financial advice.

The Right Choice

Think back to the last three financial decisions you made. Do you think your decisions were more aggressive or conservative? Do you see a pattern?

Now go to the website below and take a moment to complete the Investment Risk Tolerance Quiz. How far did the decisions you've made recently conform to the results of the quiz?

http://njaes.rutgers.edu:8080/money/riskquiz/

Offered by the *Rutgers New Jersey Agricultural Experiment Station.*

PROTECTING YOUR ASSETS

"Confronted with the challenge to distil the secret of sound investment into three words, we venture the motto, Margin of Safety."

—Benjamin Graham

I feel what sets our services apart is the role a recovery plan plays in our portfolio design. This means the stocks, bonds, annuities and mutual funds we use to harbor your money are going to be balanced in a way that will help you reach your goals, while also ensuring the vitality of the assets over and above volatile market situations.

"Don't stop at asking, 'How much do I stand to gain?' In the same breath temper your thoughts by asking how much you stand to lose as well."

Minimizing Risk

We always customize portfolios to minimize risk for each individual investor. Investing in stocks is also an element, but we avoid chasing unrealistic rates of return that open our clients up to unnecessary risk. As wealth architects, it's our responsibility not to over-accentuate the profit-side of investing to our clients. When I'm making a decision about a financial risk, I'm not going to temper my decision by thinking about returns. Instead, I'm going to think about the ability for recovery in the event of a downturn.

This is where diversification comes in. For your assets that are on the market, you'll want to make sure you've got a safety net for when the markets fluctuate. But at the same time, if we are too diverse, if our investments are too spread out, we run the risk of not maximizing on returns over time. There are appropriate and inappropriate amounts— and ways—of diversifying,[3] and it will be different for every person, and for each investment climate.

It's hard for working individuals who are accustomed to a degree of risk in their investments to fully comprehend how different investing feels once you retire. Once you retire you're completely dependent upon the money in your accounts. Moreover, in retirement, there isn't money coming into the account every two weeks, as before. Now, instead of relying on a contribution from your paycheck, all you have to rely on is your investment returns. Your perspective will reflect this: before, you were confident and not dependent on the money, and now you're dependent upon those assets and will likely be less confident when it comes to risk.

When it comes to protecting your investments—and your meaningful life—from potential risks, don't stop at asking, "How much do I stand to gain?" In the same breath temper your thoughts by asking how much you stand to lose as well. If you're confronted with an investment choice

---

3   You can read more about this in the chapter on "Sectors."

with a certain amount of risk, and the potential return appeals to you, consider the recovery. If you can handle the potential loss, then, and only then, should you feel comfortable taking that risk.

The Right Choice

For further consideration, take a look at these questions, which will assist in determining your level of risk. They may help you get an idea of your own risk tolerance when leading up to meeting with a financial professional.

- How much investing have you done in the past?
- Do you have assets invested outside of your 401(k)?
- Do you have an online trading account?
- How much do you know about stocks and bonds?
- Have you purchased real estate in addition to your home?
- How much fluctuation in your accounts are you comfortable withstanding? (A potentially complicated question you may need professional help answering. Start out by thinking of what percentage of annual loss your portfolio can withstand over a five-year period).

LIFE EXPENSES

"Beware of little expenses. A small leak will sink a great ship."
—Benjamin Franklin

Your expenses don't just represent your spending—they represent who you are. Are you the type of person who only eats out once or twice a week or are you the type of person who takes joy in paying for your whole extended family when you dine out? Do you buy expensive items at full retail, or do you wait for them to go on sale? These may seem like comparatively small matters, but everything you do affects your life in retirement.

I occasionally get asked whether I advocate a lifestyle change after retirement. It's a question that depends on a lot of factors, but there is one thing I can say with certainty: the biggest lifestyle change I advocate is to be doubly aware of your expenses, and if you're not retired yet, it starts now. Those who are a little lax in managing their finances are more likely to feel the pinch when funds become a fixed amount.

I had my first meeting with Terrie about one year before her scheduled retirement, after which she disclosed that she had 16 credit cards from various retailers. Terrie's greatest fear was that this debt would make it impossible for her to enjoy her retirement, and that it would prevent her from passing anything on to her heirs. We had work to do. I started out by assuring her that she had options. Terrie was able to sell her investment property, which was experiencing a negative cash flow. This immediately put us on track to paying off the debt. In addition, we incorporated a structure to her plans so that she could afford long term care and life insurance. With this plan in place, she has been living life the way she always wanted.

I relate this story to illustrate how important budgeting can be, and the consequences that living outside a budget can have. Budgeting is comparatively simple, undeniably good for us, but always a challenge to actually do. A Gallup Poll put the percentage of Americans who don't budget *at all* at 68%.

There are a wealth of good budgeting websites and apps that can assist you in organizing your finances. One that is firmly established and growing in popularity is *mint.com*, which uses your account information to automatically generate a wealth of reports, tips, and suggestions to assist you in keeping on-track. I've listed a few other budgeting resources in the appendix at the back of the book, and on our website at www.miramontescapital.com.

Below are a few signs that indicate your budgeting system needs to be revisited:

- You've got a 401(k) through your job with an employer match offer, but you feel you can't contribute the maximum.

- There's no way for you to easily total your fixed monthly expenses
- You've tried more than once to accurately budget your variable expenses, but weren't able to stick to the plan.
- You don't think of the amount you and your partner make until you have to.
- Your budgeting or savings goals are erratic or they change too often.
- You're spending more than you're making!

Budgeting with Your Partner

"The great marriages are partnerships. It can't be a great marriage without being a partnership."
—Helen Mirren

If you're married or share finances with your partner, the success of your budgeting strategy is dependent upon your willingness to communicate openly about money and spending habits. Regular discussions about money with your partner may be uncomfortable at first, but if you approach it in the right way, it can form a vital pillar in your partnership.

"Attack your debt, not your partner."

A good way to go about it, which has worked with my wife and I, is to schedule it. That way, you'll eliminate the undercurrent of emotion that can sink these discussions.[4] If you only talk about money when you're fuming because your partner went on some exorbitant shopping spree or paid a bill late,

---

4   I could write another book about the art of marriage counseling through finance. I can't tell you how much I've learned about relationships from having to counsel couples who meet with me for the first time, and it seems to be their first time talking about money, too.

you'll assume the mental pattern that talking about money to be avoided because it's the time you fight. If you and your partner cultivate a financial environment where systems are in place, for the good times and the bad, you'll be effectively removing emotion from the equation. This will reduce the possibility of any discussion being construed as a personal attack. Attack your debt, not your partner.

A married couple named Bill and Mary had recently become my clients. After our first meeting, which had gone well, I got a call from Bill asking me not to mention the fact that he had amassed $25,000 in debt that Mary didn't know about. I advised him that we would need to factor a debt of that size into their financial plan. I also let him know that we could wait on that step until he felt comfortable discussing it with Mary. As we progressed through the planning process, it became crucial that the secret come out. When he finally revealed it to his wife, it was a hurdle, but they overcame it through open communication. Once the secret no longer held us back, we were able to transition smoothly into a plan that included the necessary goal of paying off the debt. The couple has now been happily retired for ten years. The reason I know they're doing well? All their accounts are now joint, and both are more aware of their expenses.

If you're finding it challenging to start up a regimen with your partner, I suggest beginning by reviewing your expenses in *"It's never just about money."* doable increments, such as quarterly. After you become accustomed to this habit, you can try moving your meetings to once every two months, and eventually to monthly.

Why We Care About Your Expenses

A pillar of our business model at Miramontes Capital is the idea that it's never just about money. The way you go about spending it represents nothing less than your life, your experiences—everything. Your spending habits *must* dictate how we advise you. Whether the retirement plan is coming from you or a financial professional, make sure that the plan reflects the realities of your spending habits.

The Right Choice

How often do you review your finances with your spouse or partner? As your retirement approaches, will this schedule change in any way?

Go to our website at miramontescapital.com and take a look at our Retirement Planning Profile download. If you don't already use something like this, speak with your spouse or partner about fitting it into your budgeting.

PENSIONS

"The goal of retirement is to live off your assets - not on them"
—Frank Eberhart

Pension plans were once noble institutions that benefited both employee and employer. When they were at their peak of popularity, the benefits they provided resulted in a working environment where employees stayed at their jobs longer, and were rewarded for it. Companies were rewarded in turn with a more experienced work force and reduced costs in hiring. Everybody won. So it's no surprise that those who have been in the work force for thirty years or more will look at pensions with a sigh of nostalgia, because things have changed. Defined Contribution (DC) plans have become more or less the norm, especially for the private sector.

Pension Payout Options

Pensions are still out there, though, and as such, I want to address a few of the considerations for you who have them on the table for your retirement. One increasingly common choice that retirees face is whether to take a lump sum payout instead of a lifetime monthly payments paid out through an annuity. Here are a few points to consider:

- When you take a lump sum, you are in control of the assets, which means the livelihood of you and your family is in your hands. There's the possibility for a greater sum down the road for increased income and for emergencies, but there is the risk of the stock market, and a danger that you can lose out if you don't handle your money correctly.

- Your lump sum payout is calculated using average life expectancies, interest rates, and income. To counteract potential disadvantages from living longer than average, you'll possibly have to make returns on the sum through investment strategies.

- You may want to put the money directly into an IRA to avoid taxes cutting into the sum.

- If for any reason you can't count on living past the average life expectancy due to medical concerns, a lump sum could be more advantageous for your heirs. If you don't have any heirs, annuities may be a good choice.

- The annuity payout is, generally speaking, for those who are risk averse. It can be considered if you're over 70 at the time of retirement.

- The lump sum may be attractive if you retire earlier, because inflation may be a bigger factor for you and control of your assets can give you the freedom to account for this.

- If thinking of the markets keeps you up at night, just choosing the annuity option can relieve a lot of undue stress.

As you can see, should you have a pension option, you may be able to position yourself at an advantage by taking a lump sum and acting wisely with it[5]. All the same, it's important to act with a plan. Receiving your pension is not like winning the Lotto. You want to make your lump sum payout work for you by being prepared, responsible, and informed.

"Receiving your pension is not like winning the Lotto. You're going to be living with the decisions you make for the rest of your life."

I had a client named Allan who was very confused choosing between the monthly payments and the lump sum. We met several times, and eventually he realized that his biggest concern was his ability to pass his assets onto his heirs. The best way for him to do this was to have more control over the money, through choosing the lump sum. We had breakfast recently, and he expressed how certain he was now, two years later, that he'd made the right decision.

Modern-Day Company Loyalty: Holding Company Stock

The loyalty to a company that pensions inspired was wonderful. Now, the climate is organized differently. Many employers do, however, make an appeal to company loyalty: the benefits package your company offers is inspired to keep you there and reward you for doing so. It is, however, important to know it intimately to ensure that you aren't unwittingly put at a disadvantage. One way this could happen is through being offered incentives to invest back in your company's stock. Pension plans, which are watched over by the Employee Retirement Income Security Act of 1974 (ERISA), limit companies from investing more than ten percent of assets into company stock. At the moment, though, there

---

5   This is not meant to be taken as specific financial advice, and is no guarantee of an outcome in your situation.

are no such restrictions for your 401(k). One study on the matter[2] done by the Employee Benefits Research Institute and the Investment Company Institute found that, of the employees who do have 401(k) assets invested in company stock, some 7% of them had more than 80% of their 401(k) tied up in company stock.

Can I tell you the odds that your company will go under, leaving you without a retirement? No. I'll even concede that if your company is a well-established one the odds are pretty small. But I can tell you it does happen. Think Enron and WorldCom. This is the all-your- eggs-in-one-basket reason for not overly concentrating your assets in company stock.

Over and above the dangers of losing money, there is the prickly situation of liquidity. Imagine you've been watching the market reports on your company's stock and have found that over the past three months its value has consistently dropped. You decide you want to sell off a portion to reinvest it, only to find that your company has a restriction[6] on employer-matched stock that can leave your money stuck. Some companies also have blackout dates for making changes, which can further frustrate or limit your ability to access your money in a pinch.

Keeping company stock while working at the company is fine. My recommendation is simply to be aware of your investments. Once you retire and you start living off your money, your stock needs to start generating real income for you. There's also the possibility that if you are withdrawing more than the dividend pays, you'd need to sell stock every month just to have an income. It's when you consider these potentials that point diversification and stop-losses (where the stock is automatically sold once it reaches a certain predetermined dollar price) become essential to protecting your future. To make sure your portfolio shifts over to a more secure level of diversity, set a target date with your financial professional for when your percentage of company stock should reach a lower, less risky level that matches your needs.

---

6   This type of restriction typically only lasts for about 1 year.

Loyalty is a good thing; and it is usually beneficial to you, too. Let's just make sure your loyalty—especially when it comes to money—is founded on solid information and planning.

The Right Choice

Take some time to make sure you are in control of all the necessary information regarding your company's benefits package, ensuring you know where to get up-to-date information on your 401(k), and policies and procedures regarding company stock options, and making changes.

The professionals at Miramontes Capital have ample experience making sense of sometimes-unclear company portals and package information, so don't hesitate to call our offices at 800-460-1595 should you feel you could use the guidance.

IRAS AND 401(K)S

"What we hope to do with ease, we must first learn to do with diligence."

—Samuel Johnson

The buzz-word "Retirement Crisis" has been circulating among financial news sources for a number of years now. Here are a number of statistics from a recent study by The National Institute for Retirement Security[3] that can provide some context:

- 45% of working Americans have *no* retirement funds at all. That's 40 million people.
- The average retirement account balance for all working Americans is $2,500, which is down from $3,000 two years ago.
- The median retirement account for Americans between the ages of 55 to 64 is just $14,500.

- 62% of households in the near-retirement age bracket have less in their retirement account than an average year's income.

Since a change in the tax code in 1978 brought about the birth of 401(k) plans a few years later[7], we've seen a swift and constant move towards the new plan in the job market. In the period from 1980 to 2008, the percentage of employees on *defined benefit,* or DB pension plans fell from 38% to 20%. And this trend isn't slowing down. The shift is still away from DB plans, where your employer is responsible for paying your pension, and toward *defined contribution*, or DC plans, where you are responsible for the investment of your money.

Much has been written on the subject of DB v. DC, and I won't take up page space rehashing the arguments. What matters is that DB pensions are impoverished, on their way out, and largely not an option for the majority of workers. Interestingly, on the employee side, an overwhelming majority of working-age people favor the current DC options available to them to the suggestion of a new mandatory government-sponsored pension plan[4].

I'm here to convince you of the dire need to get yourself into a 401(k) if you have the option, and an IRA if you don't. It may even make sense to have both. It troubles me greatly that there are still a number of people whose working situation doesn't allow for a 401(k), and yet the thought of opening an IRA doesn't cross their mind. It's easy to understand the main impetus behind their foot-dragging: *a high degree of Americans simply don't understand them.* The process is there—and I can testify to the fact that it works. The information, too, is out there in the form of books and even reliable internet sources, both of which can answer a lot of your initial questions. In fact, I believe that there is so much information available, people can be too overwhelmed to act.

---

7   401(k)s are named after that section of the Internal Revenue Code.

Some Concrete Details about 401(k)s and IRAs

In an effort to avoid overwhelming you with details, I'll offer a few simple bullet points to clarify your options. Many of you may already have one or both of these accounts.

- **401(k) Options**—Depending on your company, you'll have options when it comes to the way your contributions are invested. If you're unsure of the options available to you, or if it's been a while since you thought of it, be sure to speak with your HR department so that you can make sure you're investing in a way that makes sense for you.

- **Employer Match**—One of the things that makes 401(k)s so attractive for individuals is a company's employer match contributions. This isn't something companies are required to offer, but if it's available, do everything you can to take full advantage of it. Employers usually offer anything from a fifty cents on the dollar match for contributions, up to a specified percent (commonly 6%). Many employers even offer a dollar for dollar match. If you make $50,000 per year, your 6% contribution would be $3,000.

- **IRA and 401(k) Limits**—There are limits to the amount you can contribute annually to your plans. At the time of writing this, your IRA contribution limit is $5,500[8]. This is for all your IRAs combined, and it doesn't include rollovers from other accounts. The annual limit for your 401(k) is $18,000.

- **Catch-up Contributions**—If you're 50 or older your IRA and 401(k) can benefit from higher contribution limits. Your IRA limit raises to $6,500 total, and your 401(k) limit to $24,000. This helps if you've been unable to contribute your maximum each year.

---

8 The contribution limits here reflect the 2016 figures on the IRS website.

IRAs: Roth or Traditional?

The difference between a Roth and a Traditional IRA is that rather than being tax-deferred, as is the case with a traditional IRA, withdrawals from a Roth account are tax-free in retirement. This opens up a variety of strategies for investors.

- Because you already paid taxes on the funds put into a Roth IRA, there is no penalty for making early withdrawals for emergencies. This flexibility may make sense for some people's retirement plans. Be careful, though, because penalties may apply on withdrawals from the *earnings* the account has made. I highly recommend not acting without professional tax advice.
- Paying the taxes at the time of investment, as you do with a Roth, may make more sense for long-term investors, or investors who aren't bothered by paying taxes up front.
- Keep in mind that contributions to Roth IRAs are limited for individuals who make over $117,000 annually; and individuals who make over $132,000 are ineligible for a Roth entirely. For married couples, the phase-out starts at $184,000 and you are ineligible at $194,000. Check with a professional if you have questions about your eligibility.

When confronted with the unknown, your mind will tell you all sorts of things. The worst thing you can do is completely ignore them, assuming everything (i.e. your retirement and new beginning) will just work itself out because you didn't want to face the unknown, or simply decided you don't believe in it. All that is needed to stop uncertainty from snowballing into something uncontrollable is to find a financial professional you can trust, someone who is going to help you achieve your most meaningful life.

The Right Choice

Many of you have probably begun the process of saving for retirement in some capacity. Think about your level of preparedness and decide what the next step for you might be. Think of small steps that might improve your situation over time, whether that be ramping up your contributions to an employer-sponsored plan, or looking into options outside that if you're maxing out your contributions, or if a 401(k) isn't an option for you.

Charles Schwab has a very useful Retirement Calculator that can provide you with some preliminary figures to inform your decision making. Check it out on their website, www.schwab.com, under the retirement and planning tab.

http.www//schwab.com/public/schwab/investing/retirement_and_planning/saving_for_retirement_calculator

MUTUAL FUNDS AND ANNUITIES: HOW THEY WORK

"We think in generalities, but we live in detail."
—Alfred North Whitehead

When shopping around for investment products, there is a dizzying amount of choices. The market is full of mutual funds, which are organized and managed in a variety of ways to fit individual portfolio needs. The other major investment product, annuities, offer still more choices, with specific benefits that may be of interest. Both annuities and mutual funds are grouped investments that allow you not to have to choose each one of your stocks, bonds, real estate, etc., in your portfolio. You can consider both as a more efficient form of investing, but there are major differences. I've organized this chapter to compare mutual funds and annuities as a means of better understanding the two investment

63

types, and to see how these products may apply to your life and which may be the better choice for you.

Mutual Funds: To Manage or Not to Manage

When you choose a mutual fund, the money you invest in it is taken up by a money manager, who makes it their job to manage the portfolio of stocks, bonds, and real estate in order to create returns on the investments and manage risk. It's the fund managers' job to ensure that the fund is well-constructed and properly diversified. Choosing just one mutual fund could save you countless hours of research constructing that diversity in your own portfolio.

If you select a mutual fund for a portion of your investments, you want to make sure it's composed of good investments. Given the choice between an actively managed or passively managed fund, which do you think is a stronger investment? The word "passive" can have a negative connotation. It can make you think of a manager idly sitting by while the fluctuations of the market wreak havoc on your savings. When we look at the statistics, however, the exact opposite turns out to be true.

Morningstar, a reliable source of independent market research specializing in mutual funds, has shown continually, through studies of both products, that the more effort fund managers put into choosing their investments, the more susceptible to loss the funds become. Uniformly over time, passively managed funds tend to weather the fluctuations in the market and end up outperforming actively managed funds. What's more, their internal management fee is typically much less than an actively managed fund[9]. So why are people still choosing active mutual fund options when they are riskier, cost more, and perform worse statistically?

The answer is relative. We can compare the variety of funds out there to vehicles. All the vehicles on the market will get you from point A to

---

9   Possibly even a tenth of the price of the active funds.

point B. But you've got compact hybrids, minivans, SUVs, pickup trucks, commercial trucks, all of which accomplish different things. You'll need to look closely at your specific needs to see which vehicle matches your lifestyle

"Who would like to buy the most expensive house, in the most expensive neighborhood, at the most expensive time?"

best. Likewise, you must look at the specific needs of your portfolio.

This is another of the reasons why I made the choice to become an independent Registered Investment Adviser: it gives Miramontes Capital the ability to access significantly more investment choices with lower fees for my clients. My greatest concern has always been the well-being of my clients, and it has been refreshing to renew my commitment to helping retirees, free of the profit-driven corporate interests of a larger brokerage firm.

Diversify?

Let's say, then, that you've decided to go with a passively managed fund. The question now is, *which* passive fund? Many of the general Internet resources out there make it seem as if so long as it's passively managed, it doesn't matter. If you're still working and not solely dependent on the income, this may be true to an extent. But if you are living off the capital in the account, it absolutely, positively matters which fund you choose, and when you choose it, too.

Timing is a serious factor when we consider the type of fund to buy when markets are high. I commonly joke to investors, "Who would like to buy the most expensive house, in the most expensive neighborhood, at the most expensive time?" This is what we want to avoid doing with any investment. When you're assessing a fund, not only do you need to look at the details of the fund, but the market context as well. All mutual funds come with a prospectus, which explains the rationale of the fund, any inherent risks, and hopefully a good amount of market data. It's crucial to review this document before making any big commitments.

I also let investors know this very important principle: You make your money when you buy, not when you sell. When you sell, you're just cashing the check; your buying point dictates how big or small your profits are going to be. You're buying that potential for growth. An informed decision into which fund you're trusting is what makes the difference.

Annuities

The principle of annuities is pretty similar to that of a mutual fund: you've got people making the specific investment decisions for you. But the feel of these two products couldn't be more different. The number one word that can describe annuity products is *insurance*. Think of annuities as insurance on your investment. Annuities are characterized by a pay-out method where, after you invest your sum of money, you are given regular payouts, usually monthly.

I think one of the biggest attractions of annuities is this income stream. Individuals are paid back for their investment in a clearly defined way that resembles getting a salary from one's employer. Secondly, annuities are attractive for their ability to pass on a sum of money to an individual's heirs at the time of their passing. The regularity and dependability is certainly attractive to retirees who want reliable income, whether for themselves or their heirs. Because annuities are basically insurance for your money, it is more secure when compared to the purchase of a company's stock.

A common type of annuity retirees come into contact with is what's called a corporate annuity. This is an insurance product that your company purchases once you retire, supplying you with a fixed income for the rest of your life. They are commonly compared to the other option that your company may offer you, which is a lump sum payout at retirement.

Riders

There are also various "riders" that can be "attached" to the annuities. These allow benefits such as fixed income streams for life, or the ability to pass on a lump sum to your beneficiaries at the time of your death. One common rider is a Cost of Living Adjustment, or COLA, which automatically adds an annual percent increase to the monthly payout you receive.

Most corporate annuities *do not* come with this option. COLAs, along with other options and riders may be available on the annuity market. If you've accumulated a retirement sum of, say, $500,000, but you want more flexibility in the way that money is used, a lump sum payout can open you up to a wide variety of annuities and riders, as well as other investment options.

Fixed or Variable?

When weighing the options of other annuities, you can be offered the choice between a fixed or variable product. The difference comes from their interest rate. Given the choice, do you lock yourself into a steady interest rate that may leave your money in the dust if the markets soar, or do you have faith that possibly fluctuating market rates are going to take care of you?

Certainly, there is a level of security in fixed annuities (corporate annuities are exclusively fixed-rate). However, you're going to pay for that security over time in the form of lower returns on your investments. If you invest in an annuity that offers a 3% payout annually and you have $500,000 to invest, you'll receive $15,000 per year from the insurance company, for life, guaranteed. Once you add your social security, this might meet your financial needs, and you can rest at ease. It's just the thing for retirees who are more risk-averse, worried about fluctuations in their portfolio, and for those who have relatively low expenses and no major debt. It may also be what you want if you're significantly older than average when you retire.

If a 3% income sounds low, you may consider variable annuities, which also offer income for life in many of their choices. These may pay in the range of 5% on $500,000, making a payout of $25,000 per year. With variable annuities, your money is invested by the insurance company in what are called *subaccounts*, which are simply bundled stocks and bonds managed by mutual funds. Therefore, these accounts will reflect the activity of the markets, meaning your gains can potentially be higher, but your assets are open to a greater degree of risk. However, there are other benefits, such as optional living benefit features, that can offset some of this risk.

A variable rate annuity may sound similar to a traditional mutual fund, but they are *not the same,* even though the investments may be similar. An annuity gives you the security of an investment insurance and the potential benefits of riders, which can provide a wide variety of incentives, such as guaranteeing you'll get all of your principal back. But it also has higher fees than a mutual fund. You have to weigh the benefits and decide if it makes sense for your needs.

Other Applications of Annuities

The wealth of different insurance products out there can have their place in many specific situations. Here are a few:

- Assume you're in your mid-forties and you've maxed out your contributions to your IRAs and 401(k) for the year and you inherit $250,000. If you want to invest it in a tax-sheltered environment, an annuity product might make sense over a mutual fund, where your gains will be taxed yearly, cutting into the growth of the capital.

- If a guaranteed income is attractive to you, annuities can be designed to give the investor what's called a living benefit, which is a payout of, say, 5% that the annuitant enjoys while he is still living. For example, with a living benefit arrangement, you'll be able to receive a portion, say 5%, on an investment of $250,000 for your life, and when it comes time to pass on the money to your heirs, the sum is still there for them at $250,000[10].

- In a market environment where there is a higher level of risk, putting the stock portion of your portfolio into an annuity can be a way to buffer your investment against an impending downturn.

- If your retirement account is smaller, you have more to lose in a big market downturn. In such situations, insurance on those investments may be a good idea. You can guarantee an income so you won't have to go back to work if your account is depleted[11].

With mutual funds as well as annuities, the details need to guide your choice. You'll want to inform yourself of the details of the product you're looking at, certainly, but just as importantly, you want to be aware of the specific needs of you and your loved ones.

Take-Away Points for Mutual Funds and Annuities

We covered a lot in comparing these two types of retirement products. Here is a short list of what we discussed in this section:

---

10 It's important to closely check the guarantees of the insurance company you select for your investment, as they can change from month to month and year to year.

11 Although, the same logic can easily be applied to the person with 20 million in his account. If you're in a good position, what's the sense in risking it? But in the end, it's a matter of personal preference.

- Passive funds have lower fees than active funds.
- Passive mutual funds statistically earn more than active funds over time, generally.
- Because they are insurance on investments, annuities make sense for retirees with security in mind.
- Over time, a sufficiently diverse mutual fund will often yield better gains than various annuities generally.
- The security and variety of options that riders offer, though they come with higher fees, may suit the specific needs of some retirees.
- Corporate annuities offered through employers can have lower fees.

The Right Choice

Take 15 minutes or so to visit a site that offers mutual fund information, such as Morningstar, Bloomberg, or Seeking Alpha. Make a short list of funds that may match your situation and risk level.

Visit miramontescapital.com and click on the 'annuities' tab to review the products and information there.

http://www.morningstar.com/funds.html
http://www.bloomberg.com/apps/data%3Fpid%3Dfundscreener
http://seekingalpha.com/etfs-and-funds/mutual-funds

SECTORS—A WAY TO DIVERSIFY

"Happiness is not a matter of intensity but of balance, order, rhythm and harmony."

—Thomas Merton

Even if you know very little about investing, it's likely you've heard that keeping your stocks diversified is a good idea. Theoretically, you can't really argue against the benefits of a diverse portfolio. However, it is possible to sacrifice returns through too much diversification. This can express itself in a few ways, but something we work to avoid is blindly diversifying.

The theoretical advantages of diversifying are no excuse for closing your eyes to the information that's out there. If you do your research, have your finger to the pulse of the give-and-take of the markets, you're going to be making informed choices. We don't want to be acting on hunches or emotion, but rather, grounding our decision in methods, data, and history.

I had a client that thought (after meeting with a different financial professional) that the standard portfolio allocation of 60% stocks and 40% bonds was providing him with adequate diversification and income. After I met with him and reviewed his portfolio, we realized together that his specific income need required a higher dividend payout than he was receiving from his current investments. We began looking at different sectors to branch out into, and were able to arrive at a sector diversified portfolio that would provide him with the income he needed without requiring him to sell off shares every month to cover his expenses. A broader range of eight different sectors gave his portfolio a level of diversification that matched his needs.

"The theoretical advantages of diversifying are no excuse for closing your eyes to the information that's out there."

This brings us to the power of sector diversification. Investors think of sectors in a few different ways. You can decide to invest in industrial sectors, meaning you'd choose from utilities, pharmaceuticals, real estate, aerospace, energy, software, and others. This is a common and helpful way of thinking about the market, because it allows you to isolate potential risk when you're structuring and restructuring your portfolio. If technology is plateauing just when you get a bonus at work that you'd like to put into stocks, you may diversify differently that month by choosing real estate. Other sectors can be geographically organized. Investors may try to find emerging markets in other countries to design funds around.

Are we trying to predict the markets, which so many professionals backed by studies and statistical data say will never work? Not at all. We just want to avoid throwing our money into sectors that have a high likelihood of taking a downward turn. This isn't encouraging risk—quite the opposite: I'm advising you to keep an eye out for it and diversify *away* from it. Let's try to make our investments count by buying them at the right time.

The Right Choice

By looking at sectors, we can see what's been happening over time in an industry and make informed decisions about the future. Choose a sector you'd be interested to invest in and use *Morningstar* or *Bloomberg* to see what that sector has been up to in the past 36 months. Does this help you infer anything about the potential for gain or loss in the future?

CONSIDERING TAXES

Taxes, especially as they relate to your retirement assets, can be a source of constant concern as you plan for retirement. Due to the variety of accounts and income sources many of us have as we enter retirement, each with a potentially different tax situation, it can feel challenging to stay on top of things to ensure that you aren't paying too much or too little. This is why so many of us enlist the services of a tax professional.

Discussing specific tax situations is beyond the scope of this book, simply because the vast range of income sources and accounts, as well as the changing nature of tax code and the unique financial situation of every individual, means the list would be almost endless. Rather, with this chapter I want to introduce a perspective toward taxes and the tax code: taxes are just another aspect of one's retirement plan that every single retiree has to factor in. Moreover, there is always a tax situation that works for you. With this in mind, there are many options that can be utilized, often with the help of a tax professional, to make your portfolio tax-efficient. As a retirement planner, I make a point to work with my clients' CPAs whenever possible to ensure that the financial plan we arrive at includes the most advantageous tax options for the individual.

Required Minimum Distributions (RMDs)

If generating a monthly income from your retirement account is not a concern for you, it would be great to leave all that money in your IRA continue to grow, leaving you with a substantial estate to pass on to your heirs. However, the IRS has systems against this—there's a law mandating required minimum distributions (RMDs) from the account. From the IRS perspective, it's understandable—they've allowed the money to go on in a tax-deferred state for the duration of your working years, and they want to ensure that the income is taxed in a predictable way.

RMDs are relatively simple, but very important to get right. Once you reach the age of 70 ½, you have to withdraw a certain amount from all of your IRAs or face steep penalties. Using what's called the Uniform Lifetime Table, which is generated based on life expectancy, you find your current age and arrive at a corresponding approximate number of years that you'll live, which will stand for the distribution period of your IRA assets. Say you're 70 years old. Your distribution period will be 27.4 years[12]. To calculate the minimum distribution of that year, you'll take the total amount of your IRA and divide it by the distribution period. If the account had $200,000, this divided by 27.4 gives us a required minimum distribution of $7,299.

---

12   From the 2015 Uniform Lifetime Table, available at IRS.gov

Age	Estimated Life Expectancy	Amount in account	Account Divided by Life Expectancy
70	27.4	$200,000	$7,299

If you have a sufficient income to live comfortably on from other sources like Social Security, conforming to the RMD rules can feel burdensome. However, just as with taxes in general, RMDs are simply another aspect of the normal retirement landscape, something that you and your retirement professional need to discuss and work into your retirement plan.

Do I Have to Wait Until 59 ½?

A very common question that clients ask me regards the penalty for tapping into your retirement accounts before the standard age of 59½. The thought of losing another 10% of their hard earned retirement funds to the IRS is enough to keep most people from even considering taking the money out early—but is there a way?

One recent client of mine needed to retire at 58. I met with his CPA to discuss the possibility of the client taking an early distribution from his retirement account. We reached the decision that taking out early payments could work for him through filing a 72(t), a plan designed by the IRS to allow individuals to withdraw "substantially equal periodic payments" for a set amount of time, while avoiding the 10% tax penalty. Using this, we constructed a plan in which he could withdraw a certain amount each year over the next 5 years. He remained on-track financially, and was able to build his retirement in the way that made most sense for his family.

A Substantially Equal Periodic Payment, or SEPP plan, though relatively straight-forward, is still an exception that is not for everyone. Certain factors, such as needing to retire before previously planned, or having debts that may be burdensome to pay off, may make a SEPP plan a good option. It's important to remember that very specific guidelines must be met regarding the payments, which depend on the way you choose to set up the SEPP exception. One rule to keep in mind is that the payments need to continue for at least five full years, or until you've reached age 59½. This means if you start drawing on the account when you're 50, you'll need to continue receiving the payments until you're 59 ½. Only pursue a SEPP exception with the guidance of a financial professional, and possibly a tax professional as well.

The Right Choice

After considering the two tax situations mentioned in this chapter, assess the tax support that you will have during retirement, including CPA or tax professional and/or retirement planner. Do you feel that the amount of resources available to you is sufficient for when you enter retirement? If not, consider next steps to take.

LONG-TERM CARE
AND LIFE INSURANCE

More people are realizing that long-term care is a possibility for them and/or their loved ones. As a result, long-term care insurance policies are more commonly included in the average person's plan for retirement. Here are some statistics about long-term care in America:

- If you're 65 or older, you have a 70 percent chance of needing some form of long-term care during your remaining years.
- The average length of care needed for women is longer than that for men, at 3.7 years and 2.2 years, respectively.
- 20 percent of seniors will need care for longer than 5 years.[5]

America is an expensive country for long-term care. It can therefore be very sensible to look into different insurance plans.

There are two types of long-term care plans companies offer. The first type of policy charges a monthly premium in exchange for a predetermined monthly coverage, for a set number of years. One such plan might have a $250 monthly premium and in turn guarantees to pay $2500 monthly payouts for a set period of 48 months. Another type of long-term care coverage allows you to deposit a lump sum of money, giving you access back to this principal at a determined time, say in 5 years, if you do not begin using the plan. For this, you would then be able to receive a predetermined amount of coverage, such as $2500 per month for 48 months, in the event that you need long-term care. The distinct advantage here is that you don't have to concern yourself with monthly payments, and you'll get the original investment back if you never use the long-term care. Both options have the ability to work well for clients. Both offer what you need, when you need it most: assets to cover steep medical costs, which most would find difficult to cover without the insurance.

Life Insurance

It's an unfortunate truth that life insurance is misunderstood by many soon-to-be retirees. The most common misunderstanding is thinking that life insurance is limited to people who need it to provide an income for their partner. However, there are a few other situations where life insurance can really make a difference.

Maria was a client who had an estate of $10 million at the time of her passing. Because of the size of her estate, she had a tax bill of about a $1 million that her beneficiaries would have to pay. So she bought a $1 million life insurance policy, thus covering the tax responsibility her heirs would have been left with and ensuring that they got their full inheritance.

I had another client named Francois, who had debts totaling $50,000. He was concerned that when he passed away he would be burdening his beneficiaries with this debt. We were able to set up a plan that included a $400,000 life insurance policy in order to make sure that the future of his estate didn't include a burden for his beneficiaries.

In many situations, both long-term care *and* standard life insurance policies can benefit clients in their plans. Increasingly often, at least one of these products may be needed to safeguard retirement assets against the unexpected, and to ensure that your loved ones receive everything you've prepared for them.

The Right Choice

Do you feel that a long-term care policy is a feature you'll work into your retirement plan? If you have reservations, take some time to look over the information provided on longtermcare.gov, which provides a good amount of resources for individuals considering this option.

REAL ESTATE
INVESTMENT TRUSTS (REITS)

Have you ever bought a shopping mall? Or a sky scraper? It may seem out of reach, but I've helped many average investors benefit from owning real estate just like this. The key is Real Estate Investment Trusts. REITs make it possible for regular people to invest in large, often commercial properties in a way similar to investing in a company by purchasing shares.

Not a Fixed Income—But an Income

The number one thing retirees are usually after in their investments is a secure, dependable source of income. REITs are required to pay out 90% of earnings. This may make them appear to be stable compared to other investments. However, it's important to remember that they are basically real estate stocks, and as such, their gains fluctuate with the markets. However, REITs pay out dividends, and although the payouts may fluctuate, it can still contribute to a steady stream of income. Here are some other points to consider:

- **Solid Transparency and Governance:** The REIT industry consistently gets high ratings for transparency and governance from independent consultants.
- **A good way to balance your portfolio:** REITs gain and lose separately from, say, the S&P 500. They can therefore help reduce volatility in your portfolio.
- **Taxes:** Dividends from REITs are taxed as ordinary income. However, REITs can be incorporated into IRAs and 401(k)s to at least provide a tax-deferred situation.
- **Non-Traded REITs:** Be careful to avoid REITs that are not publicly traded. For one, they are less liquid, which leads to less transparency: it can be hard for investors to find out what they're worth. Second, commissions are high, and they usually don't earn as much as the publicly traded REITs.
- **Funds are a good choice**: You can find individual REITs on the market, but a strong REIT fund may reward investors with diversification and stronger returns.

Different Kinds of REITs

Let's take a look at some of the variety available to you on the market.

Mortgage & Equity REITs: Many will choose to invest in REITS by purchasing shares on the market. There is one distinction that may influence your decision: Equity and Mortgage REITs. Equity REITs are comparable to a real estate company, whose job it is to lease, maintain, and develop property in a way that increases the overall value of the REIT. Mortgage REITs, on the other hand, are lenders. They extend credit to real estate owners in order to make profit.

These two types of investments can be found on the New York Stock Exchange. Some REITs concern themselves with only one type of property, like healthcare or apartment buildings, while some embrace a variety. REITs can own property solely in the United States, or internationally. Taking a little time to research will yield a variety of investment options.

REIT Index Funds: The second common way that investors utilize REITs is through choosing an index fund that focuses on them. This mutual fund product selects from a variety of REITS, giving you more diversity. REITs tend to perform differently than other company stocks, so even if you have a mutual fund, a REIT index fund can add further diversity to your portfolio.

The Right Choice

As a point of interest take a look online at reitsacrossamerica.com to learn a little more about the REITS market in your state, and to see a sampling of buildings you probably never knew were REIT-owned.

HOW MUCH SHOULD
I BE PUTTING AWAY?

"Paralyze resistance with persistence."
—Woody Hayes

For anyone just starting out on the savings process, the natural question you want to ask is, "How much should you be putting away?"

This is a very personal question that evades a one-size-fits all answer. Instead, we'll run through a simplified scenario to make you aware of the overall process. I'll remove compound interest, which is a huge factor in your retirement savings. I am also going to avoid factoring in returns gained from investments, which we would expect to grow our assets by 7% or more over time. My purpose is to simply show you the difference made when you put away a little more than the bare minimum. The average individual puts away 5% of their income into their 401(k). Many financial institutions advocate putting away 10% of your annual

84

income to prepare for retirement. But what happens if we put away 15%? Let's calculate the three scenarios:

- Let's take an average annual income of $60,000 and let's say we start saving at 30
- At 5%, we'd be putting away $3000 every year, and retiring at 65, we'd have a total savings of $105,000. Certainly higher than the average savings of $14,500!
- Now take that simple amount and divide it by the years we'll expect to live, let's say another 20. That gives us an allowance of $5,250 per year.

It's good to note here that our savings is lunch money without investments and the help of interest. (If we include compound interest and an average 7% return on investments we'd arrive at $1,055,305!) Let's now compare this scenario with the other two:

Annual Income	Percent saved for retirement	Years saved	Total savings	Annual retirement income	Sum After Compound Interest & 7% Investment
$60,000	5%	35 years	$105,000	$5,250	$1,055,305
$60,000	10%	35 years	$210,000	$10,500	$1,470,016
$60,000	15%	35 years	$315,000	$15,750	$1,884,726

Thus putting away 5% more annually leaves us with a sum $5,250 greater, or in percentage terms, *a 100% increase* over the initial amount. (With compound interest the sum was $1,470,016, an increase of over

$400,000 dollars). With a savings of 15% the numbers continue to grow. As you can see, every extra dollar that goes into your retirement account will end up being much more than a dollar—not spiritually or emotionally, but mathematically.

One Marshmallow or Two?

I'm reminded of a famous sociology experiment done through Stanford University in the 60s. A group of children were given the option of eating one marshmallow immediately, or, if they could wait a short time for it, get two marshmallows. The outcome of the experiment was astonishing. The sociologist tracked the kids into their adulthood and found that the kids who were able to exercise self-control showed greater success in other factors of life, including significantly higher SAT scores and healthier Body Mass Index. These results suggest that if you cultivate in yourself (and your kids) a tolerance for delayed gratification, greater rewards in many areas *will* be yours.

Consider Your Annual Income

Let's think about the question in another way: How much do you need, in multiples of annual income, to have adequate retirement funds? Our models above, based on $60,000 annually, only had 3.5 times the income, and it was basically untenable. There are a variety of models out there. A variety of other financial professionals have proposed 8 times a person's annual income, or $480,000 for a $60,000-a-year household (I still find this figure pretty conservative). Still other

> *"Every extra dollar that goes into your retirement account will end up being much more than a dollar—not spiritually or emotionally, but mathematically."*

models give figures like 11 times, or even 25 times the household's yearly earnings[13].

So as you see, there is just no easy answer to this question. We've got a truck-load of variables to take into account, because you and the person living in the house next door are completely different people; you and your spouse are different people; and yes, even you in your 40s, you in your 50s, and you in your retirement years are likely to be considerably different people. This is why my staff and I monitor our clients' accounts so much!

If we return to basics, there are essentially two ways to become wealthy:

1. By spending significantly less than you have.
2. By saving significantly more than you spend.

It's that simple. Above all, remember that you don't need a massive amount of capital to be comfortable. Listen to what your budget tells you about your needs. This will tell you how much you should be putting away.

Take-Away Suggestions for Retirement Savings

To boil all the scenarios and recommendations above down to a few bullet points[14]:

- Putting away 10% of your earnings for retirement is a good start, but likely not enough. Rather, aim for 15-18% annually.

---

13 The huge difference in figures here is due to variables, like rate of return on investments both before and after retirement, inflation, and income after retirement.
14 These recommendations are by no means intended as specific advice, and don't guarantee a successful outcome. Life is more complicated than that.

- Cultivate a mindset where you acknowledge the positive results of delayed gratification. You want two marshmallows, don't you?
- As our "simplified" model showed us, without some return on our savings, we'll likely be in trouble when it comes time to retire. Aim for equity investments that gain at least a 7% return. And keep in mind an average inflation figure of 3.5%.
- Start saving now! These numbers really only work if your savings plan is adhered to for 25 years or more.

The Right Choice

Run through a simple scenario of savings based on your income. If you regularly put aside a certain percent, see how much more you could end up with by increasing it a few percentage points.

Charles Schwab has a good online Retirement Calculator to assist you:

http://www.schwab.com/public/schwab/investing/retirement_and_planning/saving_for_retirement/retirement_calculator or visit our website Book tab for a direct link.

SOCIAL SECURITY

The most recent data[6] from the Social Security Administration (SSA) states that over 59 million people are currently receiving benefits. In their own words, the SSA envisions Social Security as 40 percent of a worker's income. This is a fact that must have escaped the participants of a recent survey, where 36% of soon-to-be retirees said that they planned for social security to be their main source of income in retirement[7].

The average monthly payout per beneficiary is $1,219.04. If that is enough for you, then Social Security will work for you. But if you are anything like me, you'll agree that living on social security alone isn't enough, especially if you want to have a comfortable standard of living that allows you to branch out a little, and won't require alternative sources of income[15].

---

15 Interestingly, that same survey said that 59% of participants in their 50s planned to work past age 65 or not retire at all; what's even more interesting is that the report found that in the 60s age bracket, this number skyrocketed to 82%. The reason, to my mind, must surely be that the group of workers, who in their 50s said they wouldn't need to work, in their 60s found they had to.

If the numbers alone aren't enough to persuade you to think beyond the check you'll be getting, the future of the program holds other worries. I don't buy into the hype that Social Security is going bankrupt. All the same, the prospects of the program continuing at full capacity are dwindling. The Social Security Administration's own calculations state that under current conditions, funds for payouts may become fully depleted by 2033[16]. But before you and your neighbors do something irrational, realize that even worst-case scenarios aren't catastrophic. Should the problems not get fixed politically, beneficiaries would see a reduction in benefits—not a cancellation of them.

What do I recommend, then? Don't discount Social Security; as an institution, it likely isn't going anywhere for many decades. But you want to recognize that the types of benefits you'll be getting are just that: a benefit. That's why they don't call it Social Security livelihood.

Social Security Strategies: You've got Options

For the amount of possible choices you have with Social Security, it's amazing how little information people actually go on when making decisions, such as when to start collecting benefits. Other possibilities, such as deferring benefits, spousal benefits, and survivor benefits, can add a further need for strategy and informed decision making.

When can I start collecting?

The age at which you can receive full benefits is currently 67 years[17]. The earliest you start collecting is age 62. At this point, you would see a 30% reduction in your payouts. Each year you wait, the amount your payouts

---

16 How this is possible is not important for us to fully understand, but can be quickly summarized by the cyclical nature of the collection and payouts the system has. Current retirees are receiving the contributions made by current workers, and in turn, current workers will receive the money of the next generation of workers.

17 These and the following are the 2016 figures, taken from socialsecurity.gov.

are reduced is lessened. The same is true for collecting your spouse's benefits. 62 is the earliest you can collect, but you'd receive only 32.5% of your spouse's payouts. If you wait until 67 to collect on your spouse's benefits, you'd receive the maximum possible amount of 50%.

When should I start collecting?

The decision of when to start collecting is a very important one—but for different reasons than you might have thought. I'm going to suggest that we worry less about maximizing our returns and more about maximizing the usefulness of those returns.

I've had many clients make the choice to begin receiving benefits at a younger age to supplement their income. They felt they needed to have more retirement funds available to them, and that made sense and worked for them. Likewise, I've had just as many clients with significant amounts of capital on hand, allowing them the ability to wait to take social security when the payouts were at their maximum. There is no one right road to retirement.

There's a tendency for even very good financial professionals to overlook one simple but important thing: *their client!* In a somewhat robotic way, they focus on one thing: how to mathematically maximize your investments over the period of time equivalent to the average life expectancy[18]. This may work for some, but if they're ignoring your personal situation, your needs and expenses, they're opening you up to potential problems down the road. The decision of when to take social security certainly depends on your specific situation.

"We should worry less about maximizing our returns and more about maximizing the usefulness of those returns."

---

18   If it's this time during their interview, they may look up briefly from their charts to check whether you are a male or female.

My client Rob is a great example of someone who benefitted from taking social security earlier. When Rob retired, it soon became apparent to him that his retirement account couldn't support the lifestyle he enjoyed while working. The goal became to protect his retirement account from being depleted quickly, and the most expedient way of doing that was to start taking social security. By taking the benefit early, he was able to take a significantly smaller withdrawal from his account. This allowed the assets in his retirement account to grow to give him additional capital for the rest of his lifetime.

Yet another client's example shows that taking social security later on can also be beneficial. Henry was a senior-level manager at a Fortune 500 company. Because he had a significant amount of wealth accumulated through his pension and 401(k), his lifestyle was not in danger of depleting his retirement account. He maintained his pre-retirement lifestyle and was able to hold back on taking his social security until the age of 66, when his payouts were larger, which enabled him to reduce the income coming from his retirement account. Now he will be able to leave an inheritance to his heirs without sacrificing his lifestyle.

One of the factors upon which the decision depends most is your expenses. Most people can expect their expenses to increase incrementally for the first fifteen to twenty years of retirement. Then, as they become less active in their 80s, I've noticed for most of my clients a steady, continual reduction of expenses. Therefore, there may be some logic to ensuring that you have the capital to allow for actually enjoying that first decade or so of retirement. Let's run a scenario comparing the total earnings if you were to take out Social Security at 66 years old to the total earnings were you to do it at 62.

Let's say your benefits for retiring at the normal age of 66 is $1,900. If you receive your benefits early at the age of 62, the amount will be reduced to $1,400. You'd be receiving four years, or 48 months of benefits from 62 to 66. If we multiply this by $1,400, we get a sum of $67,000 in benefits, money you wouldn't have been receiving if you'd waited. Our next question is how long it will take us to get this much money from our payouts that started at the age of 66. The difference between $1,900 and $1,400 is $500. If we divide the $67,000 sum by $500, it gets us 134 months. Divided by 12, that gets us to about 11.2 years.

Tracking Difference in Earnings For Social Security Payouts Over Time		
	Collect at 62	Collect at 66
Monthly Payout	$1,400	$1,900
Social Security Earned to-date at age 66	$67,000	$0
SS earned to-date at age 77.2	$254,800 (182 months of payments)	$254,600 (134 months of payments)
It takes **11.2 years** to catch up to the earnings of the retiree who started collecting at 62.		

This means the age at which we will go into profit mode—the age we begin to make more than if we had started collecting payments at 62, is 66 + 11.2 = 77.2 years of age. That is when the earnings of the 66-year-old you will actually surpass the earnings of those who opted to start collecting at 62.

A lot of you are probably thinking, "That's it? That's the big difference?" I have plenty of clients who make the choice to take the benefits before their time of maximum payouts. These people use the money to start their retirements off. They travel while they still feel active, or wrap up home renovations that they've been putting off. In this way, holding off on collecting may not have as great an effect on your retirement as you may think. I therefore have no problem recommending clients start receiving benefits early if they feel that the money could be useful to them. For people who can guarantee that they're going to live on into their nineties and beyond, perhaps that's exactly what they want—the absolute most profitable option.

Regardless, the optimal time to start collecting from Social Security should depend on your situation. The SSA's own website says exactly that: "As a general rule, early or late retirement will give you about the same total Social Security benefits over your lifetime."[8] In this case, the number one factor in your decision-making should be the *you* side of the equation—when you feel you'll most benefit from the payouts.

It's important to seek advice in this matter, but more important to be a part of the decision-making process. There are resources that make it easy to view your payout options so you can make an informed decision. The AARP website has a benefits calculator that can assist you with making your strategy (see the Resources section at the end of the book or our Book tab on our website for a direct link). And don't forget to look honestly at your life and your needs. Don't let somebody factor you out of the equation just so you can receive a marginal profit, especially if you're not really able to enjoy it.

Take-Away points about Social Security
Here are the main points from the section:

- Most people will not be able to rely comfortably on Social Security alone to cover their expenses. It's only designed to be about 40% of an individual's average working income.
- For most people, collecting early or late doesn't dramatically affect the amount of benefits they receive over their whole retirement.

- Think about when you'll want to use that money most. Most people's expenses increase at the beginning of retirement and begin to taper off after fifteen to twenty years.

The Right Choice

Based on the principles discussed above, do you think that you'll take your Social Security payments at the average age? How central will the payouts be to paying your monthly expenses? Do you anticipate any larger expenses, such as debts to pay off or large purchases? Use the answers to these questions as a basis to form your preferred scenario.

Check the resources on the Social Security Administration's website at ssa.gov to help you decide.

INFLATION

It is very easy to paint inflation in a negative light. There a lot of people who feel abused and hurt by inflation, and a whole lot of misunderstanding. I want to address and dispel any irrationally overinflated[19] sense of wrong individuals may feel.

Inflation is a constant. It's the product of an economy that operates on supply and demand. There are two ways that inflation happens: the first, *Demand-Pull Inflation*, is when demand rises too quickly for a country's production to keep up. The other is called *Cost-Push Inflation*, which is when things like rising wages or increased cost of materials prevent companies from producing at the same rate and price. This makes for a reduced supply and therefore an increase in overall price. Inflation is measured by economy-wide indications such as that of the Consumer Price Index (CPI), not by the rise in price of a single product or sector.

---

19   Pun intended

Some decades see higher inflation[20], but the average rate for the past century, from 1913 to 2013, is 3.21%. But Sid, you might say, does that mean I just have to count on losing out on 3%, maybe more, of my hard earned, hard saved cash? Well, let's take a look.

The Two Sides of the Cash Register

Most people look at inflation from the point of view of the cost of living. If you're simply a consumer, if you only live on the "buying" side of the cash register, then yes, it's easy to feel abused. If you regularly buy a can of soda for 75 cents, when the price of the product eventually rises and you now have to pay 80 cents, you're at a loss of five cents. But consider the consumer who also has stock in the soda company. When the price goes up, he's sharing in the profits generated by the increase. When you invest in a broad variety of sectors and companies, there is a high likelihood that over time, your profits are going to double, triple, or quadruple the percentage of inflation over time. If you're invested in Apple or Samsung, when the new version of a smartphone is released and is more expensive than the last one, you share in the profits of that company in a small way, and potentially in a large way over time.

"If your money is only on the consumer-side of the equation, you're off-balance. You need to make sure you're also on the other side of the cash register."

It's a grand yet very simple equation, of much the same kind you did in grade school: when balancing equations, anything you do on one side of the equal sign needs to be done to the other. So, if your money is only on the consumer-side of the equation, you're off-balance. You need to make sure you're also on the other side of the cash register. Any

---

20   The 70s saw a nasty rate of 7.06%, but the teens ('13-'19) hold the record at 9.8% (inflationdata.com)

investing you do offsets your consumer activity with "producer" activity, and in this way, inflation becomes a non-issue for you. So as you prepare for your new beginning with retirement, you've got to ask yourself: what kind of lifestyle do you want to cultivate? That of the passive consumer? Or will you take steps now to take control of your finances and balance your equation?

Do what you can to get yourself on both sides of the cash register.

The Right Choice

Take a look at the Bureau of Labor Statistics inflation calculator:
http://www.bls.gov/data/inflation_calculator.htm
Seeing the increase in value of $100 over time ($100 in 1999 is $142 today) should make it clear how beneficial it is to get yourself on both sides of the cash register.

ABOUT YOUR PRINCIPAL

When you look at your principal, the amount of funds in your retirement account as of today, what are your hopes for that sum of money?

If you're like most of my clients, your first response will be that your money safely gets you to where you're going. Many advisors love to tell you right away how much they're going to *grow* your account. While this is part of the job of a financial professional, many lose track of the primary objective: that *we're here to protect your money*. If your principal is not protected, there can be no investment or growth.

Your Money and Our Service

If you're seeking professional assistance, it's likely because you want guidance for your financial future. Your investment is like your child. You've watched over it diligently for twenty, twenty-five, thirty or more years, as it has slowly come to maturity. Letting a financial professional into that arena is a remarkably personal process.

It doesn't matter how educated they are, or how long they've been in the business: a professional who meets with you or calls you only once a year, which is the industry standard, is simply not able to make personalized, informed decisions that will conform to your needs. No matter who your financial professional is, it is critical for you to meet or talk with them *frequently,* especially in the beginning stages of your retirement.

Our Miramontes Method for ensuring that clients remain informed on their account starts at the first meeting and doesn't stop. Once you're a client, we confer with you 10 to 12 times during that first year, which is about once a month. During the second year, we scale it back a bit to every 45 to 60 days if the client is more conservative, otherwise we continue with the 10 to 12 communications per year via call, Skype, or one-to-one meetings. This schedule of analysis and communication with our client continues for life. We also go further with the inclusion of roundtable breakfasts, where we get to meet with and stay current on the personal lives of the people we're assisting, and also give them some time to talk together and share their experiences. We share market updates with our clients to keep them informed and educated, and promote further education with weekly videos and various other events.

We do business this way because any other way simply doesn't make sense to us. Everyone has a personal relationship with their retirement funds, and we feel that that a financial architect's relation to his client's funds should be personal, too.

Some Take-Away Points About Your Principal

The concept of your principal is a basic one, but our approach to the simple things in life often defines our success or failure. Here are some main points to remember about principal:

- The only thing more important than adding to your principal through saving is protecting it through appropriate investments.
- The only way to protect against losses in your portfolio is through active management of it, which requires a financial professional who is just as active in following up with you.

The Right Choice

You may find a big difference between the communication style of the financial architects at Miramontes Capital and the professionals you may have worked with in the past. Take a look at http://miramontescapital.com/working-together/ to learn more about how important communication is to us.

DESIGNING YOUR PORTFOLIO

Even the most novice investor will agree with me: you can't treat all markets the same. So how far does a good understanding of the stock market go to building a solid portfolio? We'll postpone discussing the stock market to the next few chapters, but because stocks comprise more than half of their portfolio for many people, the question "What's your portfolio?" is likely closely followed by, "What do your investments look like?"

Your asset allocation has to be customized. The big, old-school brokerage firms are in the habit of attempting to fit all of their clients into one of a few standard portfolio models. The most common model is 60% stocks, 40% bonds. I'm not knocking it. It's a great starting point, but that's all it should be: a starting

> *"[Most advisors] stop trying to know their client the moment he or she walks out of their office."*

102

point. The fact that so many people receive this type of portfolio model suggests that the employees at larger firms stop trying to know their client the moment he or she walks out the door.

For a majority of firms out there, the customer service model still hasn't evolved to keep pace with the now firmly established advances in communication technology. There is just no reason your portfolio should have to weather the market's ups and downs when an informed professional has the power to maximize your gains and protect your downside with a few clicks.

Warren Buffet has two famous rules for investing: "Rule #1: Don't lose money. Rule #2: Never forget rule #1." This is acutely applicable to retirees. Let's say a retiree has one million dollars invested. If the market dips 10%, the new sum for that account is $900,000. Now if the markets jump back 10%, are you back to even? Not quite: the portfolio will be at $990,000. To young investors this may not be a big deal. For retirees, however, who are living off the account and taking out a monthly income, a loss of $10,000 may mean a few months of basic income just flew out the window. As such, fluctuations can hurt. This is why our clients need customized portfolios that are closely managed, to hedge them from this downside risk.

Principal Amount	10%		Principal after loss/gain of 10%
$1,000,000	$100,000	–	$900,000
$900,000	$90,000	+	$990,000

Some Take-Away Points About Your Portfolio

Here is what I suggest for your portfolio:

- Decide on your asset allocation in terms of percentages. Adhere to this ratio even in emotional situations brought about by temporary influences like stock gains and losses.
- Don't let emotions dictate your portfolio decisions.
- Don't let financial professionals who do not have fiduciary responsibility dictate your portfolio decisions: follow up and know everything that your portfolio decision makers are doing.

The Right Choice

Designing a portfolio that matches your needs is an involved process that takes time. Taking this into account, what are some questions you have for the investment style that informs how your financial professional designs portfolios?

BONDS

"Bonds, despite their ridiculous yields will not easily be threatened with a new bear market."

—Bill Gross

The concept behind bonds is a simple one: bonds are debt. A harsh fact of life is that so often it is we who are indebted financially. But a glimmer of fun in bonds is that when you're a holder of bond certificates, you're on the other end. Companies or government bodies owe you!

Unfortunately, that was the most exciting and interesting way I could introduce bonds. Bonds may not get your pulse pumping like certain stock market investments can, but these secure vehicles for your capital are an integral part to almost everybody's portfolio.

Simply put, bonds are a more secure investment because the debtor—whomever the entity—is contracted to pay to you a certain amount by a certain time. In the event that the debtor can't fulfill this financial obligation, you have a legal right to the money on your bond certificate. Compare this to stocks: a holder of stock in a company is a partial owner, and in the event of insolvency of the company, you suffer right along with them. Of course, the 'downside' to bonds is that the potential for gain is less than that of a similar investment with stocks.

Back in 2008, a lot of investors and retirees were concerned about the situation on the stock market and how it would affect their savings. Joseph, a client of mine, was no exception. To ensure that his portfolio weathered the worst of the downturn, we overweighed to a significantly higher bond ratio. When the markets suffered, he benefitted greatly, as his assets had been shielded by the bonds. This gave Joseph the safety and security he needed.

What you and your financial professional need to go through is the degree to which your principal needs to be hedged and strengthened by bonds. What's more, there is a wide range of choice out there for types of bonds, from U.S. Treasury bonds to corporate junk bonds[21].

There's No Such Thing as A Truly Safe Investment

When we say that bonds are a "safer" investment, this is a statistical generalization. It's been argued that a well-diversified portfolio with a majority of stocks is less likely to underperform than a portfolio that relies too heavily on bonds, making that portfolio "more secure"[22]. I wouldn't completely agree with that statement, but I will agree that nothing is guaranteed—even bonds. Here are some ways that bonds can underperform:

---

21 See the glossary in the back of the book for a basic overview of the most common types of bonds: Notes, Bills and Bonds.

22 I want to say that for clients of Miramontes Capital, bonds do well, since we are in the business of retirement where clients want or need the security. Many of our client portfolios are structured with a healthy amount of bonds (the average for all our clients is around 45%).

- *Interest rates can rise,* which undermines the value of the bond should you wish to sell it. Short-term bonds, which have a shorter time to mature, are less affected by this.
- *The debtor can default.* Nothing is guaranteed. If an entity with whom you hold a bond defaults, there is a slight chance you may not get your interest or even your money back. With bonds, too, there are safe investments, like treasury bills from developed countries, and less-safe investments, like bonds for an unestablished company.
- *The issuer's credit rating could fall.* If this happens, the overall value of the bond falls with it, making your bond a harder sell. More on this in the next section.
- All things considered, bonds just don't have a way of producing the same gains as stocks.

To be fair and balanced, the benefits of bonds are real. Here are a few:

- Bonds have significantly less risk involved than stocks.
- Bonds can generate yields in a predictable way, because bonds have a set date of maturity, or when your investment will be repaid. Creating a portfolio with a mix of bonds with both short and long rates of maturity can produce an income.

Taxes on Your Bonds

Because some bonds are government-issued, there are a variety of state and federal tax exemptions. Look into the tax situation of the bonds you become involved with. For instance, most municipal bonds, issued by states, counties or cities are tax-free! But this tax benefit isn't advantageous for everyone. Typically, the higher your tax bracket, the more *muni* bonds make sense, after you factor in their comparatively lower yield.[23] Additionally, capital gains taxes apply to interest gains from all types of bonds when they're traded on the secondary market, thus reducing their value to you, should you need to sell them. Remember too that tax-deferred IRAs always offset tax considerations until you are ready to start drawing on the account.

Some Take-Away Points about Bonds

- Bonds alone aren't going to rocket your portfolio above the growth you need to retire, but they add security to your investments, protecting against possible market fluctuations.
- Bonds can be comparatively less liquid than stocks, should you need access to money.
- Think about the range and types of bonds you're investing in. Don't trap your money in bonds with overly long-term rates of maturity if your plan doesn't allow for this.

The Right Choice

Is your use of bonds in your portfolio—or lack thereof— in need of a rethink? Be sure to be aware of the ways in which bonds are at work for you, and if they aren't, try to envision applications you might have for them in the near future. You can always call us for an FGA to give you an idea of how bonds can work in your portfolio.

---

23   Meant as general advice. Make sure to consult with a professional before you start buying and selling.

STOCKS AND THEIR MARKET

Investing shouldn't be based on emotions, but that doesn't mean it shouldn't be fun either. It's a beautiful feeling when the stocks you're holding are doing well. It's fun to see tendencies over time and make decisions and form strategies based on them. It's rewarding to nurture your portfolio from birth and see it mature over time. Like gardening, if done with the proper mindset, tending your stocks will provide you with a meditative, Zen-like state of acceptance. You rejoice in bounty, accept down-markets, and overall gain a connection—as the gardener has to his or her garden—to our nation's system of production.

To those who have been skeptical of putting their money into stocks, I have just two more points to make in defense of investing. You know that there has been a lot of negative feeling in recent years about investors and Wall Street. The person who doesn't invest could easily suppose that putting money in the stock market is something greedy people do, something that should be reserved only for the reckless and ambitious, or otherwise privileged—the 1%. But if we all enforce this paradigm, if fewer and fewer people from the middle class and lower are investing, that's going to spell disaster—to the middle class when it comes time to retire, but to the economy as a whole, as well. This has implications far outside the sphere of retirement. A recent survey found that more than half of people avoid the stock market entirely[9]. And I bet you can guess the number one and number two reasons for those people choosing not to: not having the money and having a lack of knowledge about investing, respectively.

When you're ready to start delving into the stock options available to you, it can be hard to know where to begin. How do we tell the difference between a good investment and a bad investment? I'll cover some of the basic ways of classifying stocks, both of which have to do with just how much risk is involved in a given investment.

How Big is the Company?

If you want to determine how much up and down is likely for a stock, look at the size of the company. The common way to distinguish this is market capitalization, most typically referred to as "small-cap," "mid-cap," and "large-cap" companies. When we compare a multi-billion-dollar company (large-cap) to a company that has just begun to be publicly traded (small-cap), the larger, more established companies will have less fluctuation and less risk. Small-cap stocks attract investors who are looking for an investment with higher growth potential.

If you've just retired, which investment is going to make more sense for your portfolio? Security-minded retirees, especially those who are depending on their retirement accounts for income, are going to gravitate toward the security offered by large- and mid-cap stocks. Another incentive that pushes retirees toward established companies are dividends. These payouts, which can amount to a more or less steady stream of income, aren't paid out by every company. The more established a company is, the more likely it is to pay out dividends to its shareholders. These dividends are yours to do with what you will—even reinvest them in the company, which many investors do. These payouts (which are often paid out quarterly) can also fit nicely into a retiree's income plan. This is where guidance and education becomes invaluable.

Growth or Value?

Investors also describe the risk of a particular stock by referring to it as either a *growth* stock or a *value* stock. Companies that are on the rise, and who are expanding in their particular market at an above-average rate are growth stocks, and have greater chance for gain. Examples of these are industry redefining companies with new products, such as solar power companies or the real estate app Zillow. This potential growth, of course, comes with a higher level of risk.

Value stocks are defined as a stock with a lower price when compared to other investments in its sector (think, "Wow, what a value!"). An investor would choose this stock because he or she thinks that the stock is being undervalued, or has more to offer than its price suggests. The details of this type of investment may show it to be solid (i.e. it has a relatively consistent earnings history). Value stocks may also boast a high dividend yield, which can again make them of interest for retirees.

Having an abundance of any one of these in a retiree's portfolio can open them up to undue risk. From comparing growth and value stocks, we see that risk level is a necessary factor in evaluating what is right for our portfolio. Other incentives such as dividends may further attract us toward this or that investment.

Emotions

Investment decisions can often be influenced not by educated decisions, but by emotion. DALBAR, Inc., the nation's leading financial services market research firm, goes about illustrating this in a thoroughly systematic and scientific way each year by publishing a document entitled the Quantitative Analysis of Investor Behavior, or QAIB[10]. The lengthy report can be summarized more or less in a few bullet points:

- People get emotional and make poor decisions.
- People tend to buy high and sell low (due to emotions).
- Emotions cause people to move their stocks around too much.

The implications for the average retiree who depends on sound financial advice to protect his or her livelihood are clear. In the sensitive financial time of retirement, having a financial planner whom you trust, who educates and empowers you, and importantly, one you are able to talk with regularly, will make the difference in your investments.

Final Thoughts About Stocks & Their Market

No matter how accustomed you are to investing in the stock market, it can be a challenge to make it fit into your portfolio in the right way. This is why my team and I have spent so much time perfecting our service model to be able to actually deliver with the support and advice you will need. If you feel that you're ready to move to the more specific stage of investment planning, don't hesitate to give our team a call.

The Right Choice

No matter how experienced (or inexperienced) you are with stocks, think of a few investment goals for your next year. It could be anything from allotting some time to look into a sector or market you've heard things about, or to simply establish a routine for more investing. Think big and see where this year can take you.

Feel free to use a resource like seekingalpha.com to inform your choices.

REBALANCING

I'm going to tell you a short fictional story about a young investor named Jimmy. Jimmy had dreams to be on top of all the latest financial trends and make the most of his money. So he built what he felt was a cutting-edge portfolio. His four biggest investments were technology, agriculture, pharmaceuticals, and real estate. For diversity, he invested 25 percent of his money in each of these markets. His technology and real estate stocks began to perform really well, which changed the diversification of his portfolio since the value of the other investments stayed about the same: he was now looking at a ratio of 30/30/20/20. Three months on, it was 35/35/20/10 (agriculture had a bad quarter). All was going so well that Jimmy decided to sell off his underperforming agriculture investments to put into the other high-performing markets. The rally in tech and real estate continued, pushing his portfolio to a ratio of 40/40/20.

Did you spot the investing mistake?

Jimmy's perfectly diversified portfolio went awry in two ways. First and foremost, the emotion of a stock performing well clouded his judgment. Jimmy allowed his portfolio to lean too far in one direction, opening him up to a higher rate of risk than he had originally planned for. What's more, he compared his "underperforming" stock to the one that was in a rally, judging it against that exceptional situation. As a result, by selling his agriculture stock when he did, he broke the cardinal rule of investing: he bought high and sold low! But in the cloud of emotions and possibilities, it can seem logical.

Allow me to propose an alternate plan of action for Jimmy. When his technology and real estate stock started to rise, what he could have done was sell off the portion of profit that went above the predetermined ratio he and his financial professional established, and then re-invest it to keep the portfolio diversified, a practice called *rebalancing*. It's a simple and brilliant principle that is overlooked because it can feel like you're going against what the market is telling you. Rebalancing, however, ensures financial security over time in two ways:

- It eliminates excessive risk that comes from having more money than you intended in any given sector or stock (who knows what is going to happen in real estate next month?).
- You lock in your profit, as you're buying low and selling high.

Approaching things from an overly profit-sided perspective can cloud judgment. The opposite approach, one of setting long-term goals that make sense for your retirement plan, building a portfolio with an amount of diversity that reflects that goal, and then regularly updating your investments to keep them on track—there is simple grace and beauty in this.

The Right Choice

Using the risk profile you completed from earlier in the book, look at a variety of asset allocation models from a web source like Schwab.com. Which one makes good sense for your portfolio?

WITHDRAWING YOUR MONEY: THERE'S A SYSTEM FOR THAT

What's more difficult, making a delicious meal or eating it?

Making it, of course[24]. We do our prep work, cook everything in the right order, monitor everything closely to make sure nothing goes wrong, and present it all on the table. And as fun as it may seem to cram everything into your mouth, part of the fun of having a nice meal is to feel civilized, to enjoy the product of your hard work one bite at a time.

The same principle applies for our retirement plan. Just as you systematically put away your savings and systematically invest them, your plan for withdrawing has to be just as systematic. We in the industry have a term for what you need to create, hopefully with the guidance of a financial professional: a Systematic Withdrawal Plan (SWP).

---

24   Steamed crab legs are one exception. Very easy to make, really hard to enjoy.

What Most People Do

When you retire, it feels like a party. You are probably having parties with your co-workers and loved ones. You and your spouse or partner will most likely take a trip. You'll feel happy offering to pay for everyone when you eat out with your family. All these and any number of other expenses and little indulgences pile up as you relax into your first year of retirement. It's no wonder that most retirees experience a steady increase in spending over the first five, ten, or fifteen years after they give up work. During this time, most retirees tend to look at the sum in their account as something they've earned that's always going to be there for them. Or maybe more accurately, they view it as investments that will continue to grow and take care of them forever. Still others probably just don't think of the account at all—they just figure they've got money, and therefore they keep spending it. In short, most people don't plan out their spending in relation to the amount they've got in their accounts. They spend according to their personal needs and desires – and that is not a good idea.

What to Do Instead

The most important element of your withdrawal plan is that it reflects the growth potential of the account. Interestingly, there is a school of thought that for most people's accounts, the number is going to be about the same. The rate of withdrawal should be around 3-5%. These numbers are arrived at through complex models that are easy to calculate thanks to computers, and you and your investment professional need only to go over your details to arrive at an appropriate withdrawal plan for you.

I congratulate every single one of my clients as they near retirement for the diligence, sacrifice, and creativity they've shown in crafting their retirement accounts. For most, if you're able to retire with a decent portfolio, it's just a matter of staying diligent and staying aware to ensure you don't outlive your funds. With a standard to go by throughout your retirement, you'll know exactly what you're able to spend and when to cut back. Then, and only then, will you feel totally comfortable enjoying the meal you've prepared.

The Right Choice

Now that we've finished going through the *Terms* section of the book, take a moment to list the top 5 things you pledge to be diligent about throughout your retirement planning process.

CHARITABLE ORGANIZATIONS

In this final chapter, I want to discuss something that can have a big impact on your retirement years both psychologically and financially: charitable organizations. Volunteering, donating, and otherwise supporting a charitable organization that is near and dear to your heart can be one of the most fulfilling ways to use the time you have in retirement. What better way to add meaning to your life than to spend time supporting a cause that you care deeply about and believe in?

But the benefits don't stop there: providing for charitable organizations can also be written off on your taxes. In Publication 526 on Charitable Contributions, the IRS outlines in detail what organizations are eligible to receive deductible contributions, and what types of contributions can and cannot be deducted.

Below is a table from Publication 526 that summarizes what charitable contributions can and cannot be deducted:

Table 1.Examples of Charitable Contributions—A Quick Check
Use the following lists for a quick check of whether you can deduct a contribution. See the rest of this publication for more information and additional rules and limits that may apply.

Deductible As Charitable Contributions	Not Deductible As Charitable Contributions
Money or property you give to:	Money or property you give to:
• Churches, synagogues, temples, mosques, and other religious organizations • Federal, state, and local governments, if your contribution is solely for public purposes (for example, a gift to reduce the public debt or maintain a public park) • Nonprofit schools and hospitals • The Salvation Army, American Red Cross, CARE, Goodwill Industries, United Way, Boy Scouts of America, Girl Scouts of America, Boys and Girls Clubs of America, etc. • War veterans' groups	• Civic leagues, social and sports clubs, labor unions, and chambers of commerce • Foreign organizations (except certain Canadian, Israeli, and Mexican charities) • Groups that are run for personal profit • Groups whose purpose is to lobby for law changes • Homeowners' associations • Individuals • Political groups or candidates for public office
Expenses paid for a student living with you, sponsored by a qualified organization	Cost of raffle, bingo, or lottery tickets
Out-of-pocket expenses when you serve a qualified organization as a volunteer	Dues, fees, or bills paid to country clubs, lodges, fraternal orders, or similar groups
	Tuition
	Value of your time or services
	Value of blood given to a blood bank

At Miramontes Capital, we have a charitable organization that is very near and dear to our hearts, which we support through contributions, volunteering and assisting with some of their programs.

The organization is Miracles for Kids, a non-profit based in Southern California that provides critically-needed support services to families with children battling life-threatening illnesses. Often times, as a result of the time and dedication it requires to treat and care for a critically-ill child, many families experience job loss, shortened work hours and reduced wages, compounded with a significant increase in bills and expenses. Miracles for Kids seeks to create stability through financial and emotional support at a time when families are crumbling from the impact of battling for their child's life.

Over the last ten years, through six core programs, Miracles for Kids has provided aid to over 1,000 families in need of support while fighting for their child's life and the stability of their family. In 2015, Miracles for Kids served 1,089 individuals throughout Southern California. As it takes a village to support a critically-ill child, the organization takes a holistic approach to family support, working hard to care for all individuals who support the ill child – including all patients, siblings, parents, grandparents, caregivers and extended family members.

The families served in 2015 live within close proximity to, or below, the national poverty level and vary in race cancer (64%), other (29%) and blood-based diseases (7%), with 50% of the total group being rare, or orphan, diseases, classified as rare and affect fewer than 200,000 Americans. Specifically in reference to the orphan disease population, Miracles for Kids is successful in meeting the financial needs of a critically underserved population of children in Southern California that is affected by orphan diseases. There is a lack of community support for this demographic and Miracles for Kids has

25   U.S. Department of the Treasury, Internal Revenue Service, Publication 526, (Washington, DC: 2015), https://www.irs.gov/pub/irs-pdf/p526.pdf.

made a tangible impact by providing critically needed financial and emotional support to this population.

Miramontes Capital is a proud corporate partner of Miracles for Kids, working together to effect change for critically-ill children and families in great need in our communities and beyond. Miracles for Kids is an excellent example of the type of organization worthy of support through estate planning, annuity giving or other intentional forms of support. We encourage you to find an organization that speaks to you as deeply as Miracles for Kids speaks to us – perhaps that organization is Miracles for Kids! – because supporting a cause that you care about deeply will enrich your life in many, many ways.

Part III
QUESTIONS AND ANSWERS

Q & A

I've included a Q&A section in this book to show the kinds of questions that often come up in the meetings I have with my clients. Even if they don't apply immediately to your situation, they may spark your mind and bring about a question you do have. This can warm you up for meeting with your financial professional, or simply give you a little more information in a more personalized form[26].

---

26 The views and advice expressed in this section are meant as general guidance; all the details of your specific situation make it impossible to guarantee a favorable outcome should you follow the advice given.

Q *A friend of mine who recently retired complained that he had had to wait a long time to start receiving his monthly income. I am going to be retiring in a few months and want to plan to make sure I am ready for this. How long do I have to wait until I receive my first payment?*

Typically, you'll have to wait 30 days until you receive your first payment. In the months leading up to your last day at work, just be sure to put aside a little extra for expenses while you wait for that first payment to roll in.

Q *What if my spouse and I don't retire at the same time? My wife has a pension and I have a variety of investments and an IRA. We would both like to retire soon, but we have some debt: about $20,000. Do you think it's a good idea for one of us to work a little longer to get the debt down before we retire, or should we use our retirement income to pay off the debt as we go?*

While there may be certain benefits to retiring at around the same time as your spouse, I'd say that perhaps only two in ten couples, maybe fewer, are able to enjoy this. There are just too many factors that influence when a person decides to retire, and very seldom do these factors match up perfectly for two partners. Perhaps with a great deal of planning in advance, matched with a consistently comfortable amount of income, you and your spouse can start your retirement together. But don't feel bad if this isn't in the cards for you.

Now onto your debt: while it isn't a significantly large amount, it shouldn't be taken lightly. Once you retire it can be easy to view your savings as a reward for all the hard work you've done over your life. In a way it is. But it's also a finite amount. And so, you want to do everything you can in your working days to secure a steady income after retiring—that's priority number one. As a result, I would seriously consider continuing to work until that debt is completely minimized. Getting a retirement income from one source and a working salary from another can be very effective in doing that. Even one year of work and disciplined repayment can greatly reduce the likelihood of dealing with that nagging debt for much of your retirement.

Another option, if continuing to work isn't on the table, is using retirement dollars to eliminate the debt. Say that $20,000 of debt is from one or more credit cards. If you're going to be paying $700 per month toward the debt, that's a serious obstacle to your monthly cash flow. Eliminating that debt up front will save a lot in interest charges, and give you more peace of mind. A financial professional can guide your decision-making more specifically by looking closely at your situation, so you may want to consider enlisting one.

Q *After reviewing my mutual fund and stock investments, I found that I have about 35% of my portfolio invested in the company I work for, a well-established biotech corporation that has been around a while. I hear all this talk about not having too much of my money invested in one place, but the truth is that the investments in the company have done really well for me. Additionally, I like the feeling of supporting my company, as it's treated me well over the years. Am I being too sentimental? Is that too much, in your opinion? And what would my options be if I want to minimize the risk of having too much in one place?*

First of all, I respect your opinion about your company and your investments. Additionally, as you say, it's worked for you. A number of advisory groups have suggested that the amount of assets invested in your own company should stay at around 10%, and more than this opens an investor to unnecessary risk. Some people like risk, and are more comfortable taking it.

I advise plenty of my clients to hold on to their company's stock if they are driven to. Not every company is in danger of becoming an Enron, which I'm sure is the example you were given. A good financial professional will place a stop loss on the account, which means they will begin selling if a stock falls below a predetermined level. This is something you can ask the person who manages your account. And of course, if you get the feeling that you should minimize the amount, you can certainly diversify in a variety of ways, but specifically how depends on the nature of your company and the investments you are holding.

For now, I'd say holding on to the stock probably won't sink your portfolio—but don't hold on forever. Once you're retired and you begin withdrawing money from the account, security becomes a priority. It's here where you can begin progressively moving your portfolio toward being more diversified and less open to risk. You can begin looking into mutual funds or ETFs that make sense for your specific portfolio and level of risk.

Q *My father wants to give me a number of stocks he has owned for a while as a gift. He's retired and currently 85. I know there are capital gains tax considerations for this that may make it better for him to hold onto them. Neither of us is in a particularly high tax bracket. What would you recommend?*

You're right about the capital gains. This is a huge factor for your father's decision. Say your father bought the stocks at $20 per share and over time they've accumulated in value to $100. This means you've got $80 of taxable income that will be subject to a capital gains tax of 20%. If we're looking at 100 shares at a taxation of 20%, you'll be losing out on $1,600. Compare this to the option of your father holding on to them. Now if the price at the time of his death is $79, this will become your cost basis. Then as the stock rises in value, say to $84, you'll only be paying capital gains on the five-dollar increase.

So there really is an advantage to your father holding onto them. He can simply will them to you, and so the cost basis, or original purchase price of the stock, will be used to estimate tax. The only reason the gift makes sense is if you desperately need the money, or your dad has some reason to get rid of them in a hurry. Your dad might be feeling, like many people his age do, a desire to unburden himself of possessions while he's there to enjoy the feeling of giving. Thank him graciously, but be sure he understands that his gift will be more efficient as an inheritance.

Q *I retired a number of years ago, although I've yet to start drawing from the 401(k). My husband still works. We want to contribute more to our retirement than the max of his 401(k). What's the best option?*

So your husband is maxing out his 401(k) at $24,000 annually if he's over age 50 ($18,000 if not). The next logical step is to look at your IRA options outside of your plan. You'll be able to contribute a total of $5,500 each, per year, or $6,500 if you're over 50. If your husband doesn't have one already, that's an easy way. Seeing as you are retired, you might have been thinking of the fact that you need an income to contribute to an IRA. If this is the case, worry not. There is such a thing as a Spousal IRA, which allows your spouse to contribute for you toward that maximum—again, that's $11,000 combined or $13,000 if you're over 50.

You'll also want to decide between a traditional or Roth IRA. For the Roth in particular, there are income considerations when you are asking about the maximum you can contribute. If you make above a certain amount ($193,000 at the time of writing this), you won't be able to contribute at all. If you are unsure which might be best for you, please consult a professional.

Q *The 401(k) plan my employer offers, which I've been putting money into for a while, is not as diversified as I'd like it to be. What is the most efficient way to spread my investments around while still remaining tax-smart?*

I think your concern comes from a good place. But from reading your question, it sounds to me like you are looking for alternatives to your employer's options, and if that's true, I'd advise against it. It's likely that the advantages to your employer-sponsored plan will outweigh any added security you'd get from an alternative retirement plan elsewhere. As such, I'd recommend you do your best to max out the 401(k) you're offered, which is an annual contribution of $18,000 if you're under 50 and $24,000 if you're over. After reaching that point you can concern yourself with adding diversity over and above your 401(k).

Now, if you're at this point already, my next suggestion might be to add diversity by opening up a Roth IRA, where you can have total liberty with the investments you choose. Furthermore, the Roth may make sense because as long as you don't withdraw from it for a period of five years after the initial investment, those deductions are going to be tax-free. A solid REIT mutual fund could be another addition that can really add security. Diversify through more, not through less.

Q *Nearly all of my retirement savings is housed in the 401(k) I contributed toward through my employer. I'm 55 and am planning to retire early to start my own consulting firm. In addition to this, I want to start getting a little income in order to pay off some debts. What's the best option?*

First of all, I'd seriously recommend running your plan by a financial professional before you start irrevocably altering your retirement accounts. That being said, your plan, although not standard, is possible—and it's good that all your assets are in the 401(k). Many people think of the age 59 ½ when they aim for withdrawing from their 401(k), because this is the normal minimum age to avoid the 10% penalty. However, a provision for what is called Separation of Service[11] exists. Those 55 or older are allowed to take either monthly payments or one-time payments yearly from their 401(k)—and again, *the 10% penalty does not apply.*

A few provisos: these are only ERISA-qualified, employee-sponsored 401(k) plans we're talking about, not pensions or IRAs. Rolling over your 401(k) to an IRA will immediately cancel out this possibility for you. Also, not every 401(k) plan allows it. Uncle Sam has made it generally acceptable, but it's still on the individual company to OK the early withdrawals. As I said, to avoid accidentally getting hit with the 10% penalty, I'd recommend having a professional check over your situation before you proceed.

Q *My husband and I are retired. Recently, we've become concerned that we're going to outlive the amount of assets in our combined accounts, and we're especially worried of this because of talk that the markets are at a high and a downturn is imminent. What kind of general advice do you have as far as making sure our withdrawal rate doesn't get too excessive? Last year we withdrew about 5% of our assets.*

This is a good question as it illustrates a common fear retirees have—outliving your money. You're probably feeling how irrevocable the change into retirement is, and how important it is to get it right. That's why having a systematic withdrawal plan is so important. It's helpful to think of your retirement accounts not as your piggy bank, something you crack open whenever a need arises, but as your income that provides you a steady stream of payments.

Using a complex system of probability modeling called the Monte Carlo method, analysts have arrived at 4-5% as an ideal average rate of withdrawal to safeguard against various problems that could arise, such as the potential market slump you mentioned. So this would be a generally acceptable number to shoot for when sitting down to budget. Guard your investments with an airtight plan, even if that means making changes to your monthly expenses. We want to avoid having to go back to work. And think, too: if you really do see an end of funds on the horizon, it's easier to work part-time when you're 65 than at 85.

Q *I'm a freelancer. Work has thankfully been successful for me over the past several years and I'm finding that I'm consistently maxing out my contributions to my IRA. What other tax-advantaged options are there for me?*

Congratulations, first of all, on being proactive in meeting your savings goals. It's great that you intuited that you don't have to be held back by the IRA limit, as some people tend to feel. Your next logical step will be one of several options (isn't it good to have options?).

Depending on your personality and level of financial awareness, you can branch out with either Exchange-Traded Funds (ETFs) if you're somewhat of a more experienced trader, or a tax-deferred annuity or tax-efficient mutual fund. From here, you can branch out further with some of the other options as needed. Happy trading!

CONCLUSION

Retirement isn't scary. But as you might be aware, the process can be. It's my hope that the facts, details, advice, and stories I compiled for this book were able to take away some of that fear of the process and replace it with understanding. With the right advice and a little creativity, you can be empowered to go forth in your retirement and make the right decisions. I also hope that you've become a little more aware of the relationship between a financial professional and his client, and you're clearer on what you want and need from that important partnership.

It's been wonderful to revisit the stories of the people I've been lucky to meet over my years in the industry. I wanted the inspirational stories included here to serve as a stepping stone for you as you make your goals and follow through with achieving them. I want to say thanks again to my clients—past, present, and future—whose creativity and love of life have made it so enjoyable to partner with them. I also want to give a special thanks to all the members of my team at Miramontes Capital. It's been a real pleasure to pursue perfection with you all.

Thank you.

APPENDIX: ADDITIONAL RESOURCES

Resources on Free Personal Budgeting

68% of Americans don't budget—at all. But even if you do, one of these great resources may help you do it more efficiently.

Mint.com

This budgeter's draw is that it links to your financial accounts, automatically transferring and updating budget information as you withdraw and deposit. Expense reports are automatically generated and sent to your email, always keeping you in the loop. There's also a nice bill pay option, among other interesting features. Best of all, it's free.

Money.strands.com

This app shares a lot of features of Mint.com, but with a bend toward financial planning: there is more to offer as far as advice, and the blog community can be a place to learn about budgeting tips. Features like a nice, clean bill calendar can at least make budgeting easier on the eyes.

AARP Benefit Calculator

The AARP has a simple tool that can help give you a basic idea of your Social Security benefits, and how they will change over time. I don't recommend relying solely on this to make your decision about when to receive benefits, but it can be a great way to answer your initial questions, and to jumpstart the planning process.

All you have to do is plug your basic personal details into the fields and it will provide charts and scenarios, as well as advice on maximizing your benefits.

Activity Log

As a retiree, you are able to take advantage of 350% more time than when you were in the workforce. A simple planner like the one below can allow you to keep yourself accountable, and ensure that you continue to be a well-rounded person. If you're able to include at least one activity from each of the categories each week, it's likely that you'll be feeling more fulfilled and productive.

Weekly Activity Log

Activities	Mon.	Tues.	Wed.	Thur.	Fri.	Sat.	Sun.
Health & Wellness							
Personal & Professional Development							
Friends & Family							
Creativity							
Spirituality							
Community Service							
Other							

RIGHT CHOICE QUESTIONS

For reference purposes I've compiled the *Right Choice* questions that ended each chapter. If you feel that someone you know may also benefit from working through them, they can be found on our website at miramontescapital.com.

Part I: Adjusting to Retirement

1. I hope you realized from the above section that the process of reviewing your finances with a professional is a personal and intimate one.

- What are some of the attributes you want your retirement planner to have?
- Go to miramontescapital.com and take a moment to look over the "Roadmap to Retirement" resource there.

2. A. Imagine you woke up in a world where all your loved ones were safe and provided for, you had no responsibilities, and you

could use your time to do anything. What would you do? Write or sketch you perfect, worry-free life.

    B. Successfully managing your time is one of the greatest keys to a successful retirement. Think about your life now. In what ways are you a good time manager, and in what ways can you use a little work? Do your answers help you perceive potential problems you may have once you're retired?

3. Create a detailed budget, including all your income and detailed expenses. Now go through your budget (preferably with your partner) and try to note down what will change about it after retirement. Which expenses will increase? Which will likely go down?

4. Discuss your daily schedule with your spouse. What about the schedule will remain the same after retirement and what will change? If you're actually nearing retirement, buy a dry erase board and map out both of your schedules.

5. Great transitions such as retirement take preparation on a number of levels. Check our website at miramontescaapital. com for a list of resources to make sure your retirement gets off to a healthy start.

Part II: Breaking It Down

6. Think about your ideal investment professional. Do you feel you can ask this person anything? Can you see yourself with this person long-term? Will the services you receive include ongoing education? Is the professional's team supportive and open to you?

    These crucial questions should inform any decision you make regarding your investment professional.

7. After considering the trust that goes into partnering with a financial professional, how do you expect your fiduciary to help you to shape and achieve your goals for retirement? For more information on how Miramontes Capital cares for your finances and your future, visit miramontescapital.com.

8. Think back to the last three financial decisions you made. Do you think your decisions were more aggressive or conservative? Do you see a pattern?

   Now go to the website below and take a moment to complete the Investment Risk Tolerance Quiz. How far did the decisions you've made recently conform to the results of the quiz?

   http://njaes.rutgers.edu:8080/money/riskquiz/

   Offered by the *Rutgers New Jersey Agricultural Experiment Station.*

9. For further consideration, take a look at these questions, which will assist in determining your level of risk. They may help you get an idea of your own risk tolerance when leading up to meeting with a financial professional.

   • How much investing have you done in the past?

   • Do you have assets invested outside of your 401(k)?

   • Do you have an online trading account?

   • How much do you know about stocks and bonds?

   • Have you purchased real estate in addition to your home?

   • How much fluctuation in your accounts are you comfortable withstanding? (A potentially complicated question you may need professional help answering. Start out by thinking of what percentage of annual loss your portfolio can withstand over a five-year period).

10. How often do you review your finances with your spouse or partner? As your retirement approaches, will this schedule change in any way?

Go to our website at miramontescapital.com and take a look at our Retirement Planning Profile download. If you don't already use something like this, speak with your spouse or partner about fitting it into your budgeting.

11. Take some time to make sure you are in control of all the necessary information regarding your company's benefits package, ensuring you know where to get up-to-date information on your 401(k), and policies and procedures regarding company stock options, and making changes.

The professionals at Miramontes Capital have ample experience making sense of sometimes-unclear company portals and package information, so don't hesitate to call our offices at 800-460-1595 should you feel you could use the guidance.

12. Many of you have probably begun the process of saving for retirement in some capacity. Think about your level of preparedness and decide what the next step for you might be. Think of small steps that might improve your situation over time, whether that be ramping up your contributions to an employer-sponsored plan, or looking into options outside that if you're maxing out your contributions, or if a 401(k) isn't an option for you.

Charles Schwab has a very useful Retirement Calculator that can provide you with some preliminary figures to inform your decision making.

http://www.schwab.com/public/schwab/investing/retirement_and_planning/saving_for_retirement/retirement_calculator

13. Take 15 minutes or so to visit a site that offers mutual fund information, such as *Morningstar, Bloomberg,* or *Seeking Alpha.* Make a short list of funds that may match your situation and risk level.

    Visit miramontescapital.com and click on the 'annuities' tab to review the products and information there.

    http://www.morningstar.com/funds.html

    http://www.bloomberg.com/apps/

    data%3Fpid%3Dfundscreener

    http://seekingalpha.com/etfs-and-funds/mutual-funds

14. By looking at sectors, we can see what's been happening over time in an industry and make informed decisions about the future. Choose a sector you'd be interested to invest in and use *Morningstar* or *Bloomberg* to see what that sector has been up to in the past 36 months. Does this help you infer anything about the potential for gain or loss in the future?

15. After considering the two tax situations mentioned in this chapter, assess the tax support that you will have during retirement, including CPA or tax professional and/or retirement planner. Do you feel that the amount of resources available to you is sufficient for when you enter retirement? If not, consider next steps to take.

16. Do you feel that a long-term care policy is a feature you'll work into your retirement plan? If you have reservations, take some time to look over the information provided on longtermcare.gov, which provides a good amount of resources for individuals considering this option.

17. As a point of interest take a look online at reitsacrossamerica.com to learn a little more about the REITS market in your state, and to see a sampling of buildings you probably never knew were REIT-owned.

18. Run through a simple scenario of savings based on your income. If you regularly put aside a certain percent, see how much more you could end up with by increasing it a few percentage points.

    Charles Schwab has a good online Retirement Calculator to assist you:

    http://www.schwab.com/public/schwab/investing/
    retirement_and_planning/saving_for_retirement/retirement_
    calculator

19. Based on the principles discussed above, do you think that you'll take your Social Security payments at the average age? How central will the payouts be to paying your monthly expenses? Do you anticipate any larger expenses, such as debts to pay off or large purchases? Use the answers to these questions as a basis to form your preferred scenario.

    Check the resources on the Social Security Administration's website at ssa.gov to help you decide.

20. Take a look at the Bureau of Labor Statistics inflation calculator:

    http://www.bls.gov/data/inflation_calculator.htm

    Seeing the increase in value of $100 over time ($100 in 1999 is $142 today) should make it clear how beneficial it is to get yourself on both sides of the cash register.

21. You may find a big difference between the communication style of the financial architects at Miramontes Capital and the professionals you may have worked with in the past. Take a look at http://miramontescapital.com/working-together/ to learn more about how important communication is to us.

22. Designing a portfolio that matches your needs is an involved process that takes time. Taking this into account, what are some questions you have for the investment style that informs how your financial professional designs portfolios?

23. Is your use of bond in your portfolio—or lack thereof— in need of a rethink? Be sure to be aware of the ways in which bonds are at work for you, and if they aren't, try to envision applications you might have for them in the near future. You can always call us for an FGA to give you an idea of how bonds can work in your portfolio.

24. No matter how experienced (or inexperienced) you are with stocks, think of a few investment goals for your next year. It could be anything from allotting some time to look into a sector or market you've heard things about, or to simply establish a routine for more investing. Think big and see where this year can take you.

    Feel free to use a resource like *seekingalpha.com* to inform your choices.

25. Using the risk profile you completed from earlier in the book, look at a variety of asset allocation models from a web source like *Schwab.com*. Which one makes good sense for your portfolio?

26. Now that we've finished going through the *Terms* section of the book, take a moment to list the top 5 things you pledge to be diligent about throughout your retirement planning process.

GLOSSARY

It's my intention to include this simple glossary as a resource for you who are starting out in the introductory stages of financial planning. Alternately, it is a supplement to add a little clarity to the overwhelming snowball of terms that soon-to-be retirees are confronted with.

To help you in your research, I've also included a number of terms that were not discussed in-depth in this book (maybe in my next one). As such, I've tried to keep the tone helpfully conversational, and contextualize the information when possible with the points I've made earlier on. I had in mind the employees that I tried my best to help in my early stages of financial advising. This is the terminology that, if they had known, would have made our meetings fruitful. May it be a resource in your lead-up to meeting with a financial professional, or as you weigh the options of various investment products on your own.

401(k) This is a retirement plan your employer sponsors, allowing you to put a percentage of your wages into an account, free of tax concerns, until you begin withdrawing from it. Your contributions to the account are also tax-deductible, usually. Keep in mind there is a cap to the amount you can contribute each year.

457 Plan If you're a government employee or other kind of civil servant, this retirement plan may be available to you. They function similarly to 401(k)s, but one key difference is that you won't have to worry about the 10% penalty for withdrawals before the age of 59½.

Accumulation Phase Compare to *Annuitization Phase*. This term comes up when talking about investment annuities. It's the period of time in which you are putting money into the annuity.

Adjusted Gross Income (AGI) Your total annual income minus deductions, credits, and other offsets, such as any contributions to your retirement plan(s).

Annuitization This is when you convert a lump sum into a series of monthly income payments for a period of time that you specify. Most often we are talking about annuities, but you may also choose to annuitize the amount in your 401(k), for example.

Asset Allocation This can be another way to refer to your investment portfolio: it's how you choose to distribute your money over the investment options available to you (stocks, bonds, real estate, etc.).

Benchmark This is what you compare the performance of one of your investments to—it's a point of reference, used to see how you're doing. You, or whomever you're investing with, may look at the Dow Jones or S&P 500 as a common benchmark.

Beneficiary IRA This is a retirement account that holds assets originally owned by someone who died, and is now under the ownership of an heir.

Bills Debt securities to be compared with *bonds*. The difference is that bills have a much shorter maturity—less than a year.

Bonds The slightly less interesting component of your portfolio, these are debt instruments sold by companies. You lend a company or other entity a certain amount and they gradually pay you back as you collect interest. Specifically, bonds have a maturity date ten or more years from date of purchase. See *Bills* and *Notes* for comparison.

Capital Gains Tax The tax that the government takes out of your profits on an investment that is sold, the year that it is sold. There is a difference between short-term and long-term capital gains in the US; short-term gains, which are 12 months or less, are taxed at a higher rate.

Coincident Indicators Various data that is meant to show the state of the economy. The Federal Reserve Bank of Philadelphia puts out decent data about the United States, including maps, monthly.[12]

Commodities What economies are built on: things of value, basic materials, cash crops, natural resources, goods and services; basically anything that is sellable and consumable.

Compound Growth Albert Einstein said, "Compound interest is the eighth wonder of the world. He who understands it, earns it ... he who doesn't ... pays it." It's an asset's exponential growth over time due to the gradual inclusion of interest.

Concentrated Fund This is a type of mutual fund where assets are overly concentrated in a small number of securities. It can also be called an under-diversified or focused fund. As you might expect, these are far more volatile than the regularly-diversified funds most take advantage of, and as such, are usually only appropriate for those with a breadth of investment information gathered by expert research and an ability to weather greater ups and downs in their portfolios.

Cost Basis This will come up when considering capital gains tax. It's the original price you paid for an asset against which the asset's appreciation will be measured.

Decedent IRA Another term for *Beneficiary IRA* (see above).

Deductible IRA When your contributions to your IRA are tax-deductible. If you aren't covered by a retirement plan at work, you can benefit from a deductible IRA.

Default Risk This is a concern for those with stock investments. It is the risk of an issuer of the stock going bankrupt, rendering your stock worthless.

Defined Benefit (DB) Plan Another way to refer to pensions. A retirement plan offered by an employer, where the company is obligated to pay a pension of a pre-defined amount to employees after retirement.

Defined Contribution (DC) Plan 401(k)s are the most common example of a Defined Contribution, or DC plan. The employer makes contributions to a plan on behalf of employees, who in turn become responsible for the stewardship of the account. The overwhelming trend for companies is moving toward DC plans and away from DB plans.

Depreciation Assets whose value erode over time, for reasons such as unfavorable market conditions, are said to depreciate.

Discretionary Authority Does your financial professional have discretionary authority over your portfolio? It's good to know, because if so, he or she can buy or sell securities without your consent. Whether or not you want this depends on your style of investment and level of trust.

Distributions This is money paid from a retirement fund, such as a 401(k), or from an asset, such as a stock or bond.

Diversification Owning a variety of assets, rather than a limited number. Diversity in your portfolio increases your security, but limits your return.

Dividend A company's net profits that are then distributed to shareholders. There is a wide variety of methods companies use for calculating dividend payouts, and alternately, companies may choose to reinvest profits rather than paying them out to shareholders.

Dollar Cost Averaging This is the practice of investing a specific, fixed amount of money into a particular investment, over time. This is a way of protecting yourself from making emotional or speculative stock decisions that would unintentionally get you into trouble.

Dow Jones Industrial Average An average of 30 of the largest companies traded on the New York Stock Exchange. One of the most common indicators of the health of the stock market.

Drift When your portfolio drifts, it means your original planned level of diversity has changed due to gains and losses over time. It's a *very* good idea to correct for this by selling off the stocks that have performed well, and so maintain the original level of diversity.

Earned Income A term for tax time, this is your compensation from wages, salary, tips, and bonuses.

Employee Benefits Security Administration (EBSA) The Department of Labor's Employee Benefits Security Administration (EBSA) is the primary agency responsible for protecting private pension plan participants and beneficiaries from abuse or theft of their pension assets. They work to enforce the Employee Retirement Income Security Act of 1974.

Employer Match Your employer may have a policy of matching your contributions to your employee retirement account.

Employee Retirement Income Security Act (ERISA) The 1974 federal law that set minimum standards for most voluntarily established pension and health plans in private industry; its main goal is to provide protection for individuals in these plans.

Federal Deposit Insurance Corporation (FDIC) The insurance agency charged with the responsibility of insuring bank deposits against the eventuality of bank failure.

Financial Industry Regulatory Authority (FINRA) The organization that regulates brokerage firms, stock brokers, and mutual funds. Their website includes a Broker Check function that allows you to search the background of investment professionals, and they offer a securities helpline service designed to help seniors.

Fixed Annuity An insurance product with a guaranteed interest rate, making them a safe, and therefore comparatively limited, investment. Interest is tax-deferred until it is annuitized and payouts begin.

Fortune 500 A list generated by *Fortune* magazine rating the 500 most-traded companies in the US.

Glide Path When you're talking about a *target date fund,* you have a mix of assets: stocks and bonds, etc. Over time, as you approach retirement, it's likely that you want this mix of assets to become more conservative or secure, meaning you have more fixed-income assets and fewer equities. The glide path is the predetermined rate at which you want this to happen. This all ends at a target date, which the glide path moves toward.

Group Annuity An option for retirement savings offered by insurance companies. This is a DB plan your employer might have established, and because the annuities purchased are grouped for all employees, the fees are comparatively lower. As we said, the momentum in the work force is away from DB plans and toward DC plans, so these are becoming less common.

Growth Stock This is an investment with a particularly high potential for growth; but with this comes greater risk.

Individual Retirement Plan (IRA) You, the individual, can establish one of these on your own, without any employer involvement. There are a variety (see below) but the two most common types are *Roth* and *Traditional IRA.* Accordingly, your contributions to the account are tax-deductible, the growth of the fund is tax-deferred, and withdrawals can be tax-free.

Industry A group of businesses that buy and sell similar goods: automotive, tech, etc..

Inflation Not as scary as people make it out to be, if you are investing to counteract it. This is more or less the natural increase in the price of goods and services over time.

Inherited IRA An IRA previously owned by a person who died where the person inheriting the account is not the descendant's spouse.

In-Kind Transfer This is when you transfer company stock from an employer retirement plan to another brokerage account when you leave the company. I recommend speaking with a financial professional if you have questions about why one might do this.

In-Service Distribution This is when you transfer assets from your employer-sponsored retirement plan to an IRA *while you're still employed*. You don't have to stop contributing to your work's retirement plan, either. If reading this piques your interest, speak with a financial professional to determine if it matches your situation.

Interest Rate Risk You may be able to guess what this one means. It's the risk that your investment's value will fall in the event of a spike in interest rates.

Liquidity If your assets can quickly and easily be converted into useable cash, they have liquidity.

Living Benefit This term comes up when thinking about annuities offered by insurance companies. It's a guarantee on whatever the annuity product, given that the provided income from the annuity won't fall below a certain level.

Market Sector This term can describe a section of the stock market whose companies are in direct competition with each other, e.g. healthcare. It can also be used to delineate the types of issuers of bonds in that market, e.g. state, corporate, etc.

Morningstar A potentially useful resource, Morningstar is an organization that provides independent investment research, and uses their huge amount of studies and data analysis to weigh in on stocks, bonds, mutual funds, etc..

NASDAQ Second in trading volume only to the New York Stock Exchange, NASDAQ is an online stock exchange allowing you to buy and sell securities.

Net Unrealized Appreciation (NUA) This comes up in tax discussions. The NUA is the difference between the *cost basis* of an asset and its current market value. Specifically, this will be important to consider when contemplating how to move around company stock. The NUA is not subject to ordinary income tax, and as a result, moving it over to an IRA would result in that amount being taxed. The other option would be to simply move the appreciated amount to a regular brokerage account. Please talk to a financial professional before doing anything you're unsure of.

Non-Cash Compensation This could include health insurance, paid time off, and any contributions to a retirement plan.

Non-Deductible IRA Annual appreciation of this IRA is still tax-deferred, but as the title suggests, you can't deduct these contributions on your taxes. You are likely only considering this option if you aren't eligible for a Roth or Traditional IRA.

Notes These are debt securities, just like bonds. The difference is the maturity rate; notes reach maturity in one to ten years.

Ordinary Income Tax term that includes wages, salaries, commissions, and interest. Profits earned from your investments don't fall into this category.

Participant Catch-Up Contribution If you are over 50, you're allowed to contribute to your retirement plan at a higher rate. Ask your employer.

Passive Fund To be compared to *Active Funds*. This type of mutual fund simply buys all the securities of a given market, in the hopes of getting returns equal to the performance of that market. Some general benefits: this is a lower-risk option and can often do better than the returns of active funds.

Pension Fund Some companies or unions pool money in order to provide pensions for their retirees.

Plan Administrator This is the party that manages the pension fund or retirement plan your company offers you.

Portfolio Drift See *Drift*.

Principal Your money! This is the original capital that you invested into your portfolio.

Profit-Sharing Contribution Sometimes your employer will base the amount that is contributed to your retirement account on the overall profits of the company. Captains of whaling boats used to do this in order to incentivize killing more whales.

Qualified Plan This refers to a plan covered by the *ERISA (see above),* and that adheres to the 401 tax code.

Real Estate Investment Trust (REIT) This type of security invests in real estate (properties and mortgages) and trades on the stock market, although there are also non-traded REITs.

Rebalancing The necessary practice of selling off the returns of investments in order to avoid an out-of-balance portfolio; what you do to maintain the planned percentage of asset allocation in your portfolio.

Re-Characterization The often complicated process of converting your Roth IRA back into a Traditional IRA; the complication comes from the need to calculate the earnings on the account for tax purposes.

Required Minimum Distribution (RMD) Generally speaking, you have to start taking withdrawals from your IRA or retirement plan account when you reach the age of 70½. The RDM is a determined yearly minimum you're obligated to withdraw. Not adhering to this rule can be catastrophic to your assets, so it's very important to make sure you do it right.

Rider A term from the world of insurance products (*annuities*), these are non-standard "add-ons" that can be used to customize an insurance plan. There are many, all helping personalize a plan in order to meet your needs. One such customization is an accelerated death benefit, which allows you to receive early payouts from your plan in the event of a terminal illness.

Rollover IRA The purpose of a Rollover IRA is to hold on to the tax-deferred status of assets that were originally in an employer-sponsored retirement account in the event that you change jobs or retire.

Roth IRA The difference between this and a Traditional IRA is that rather than being tax-deferred, withdrawals from a Roth account are tax-free in retirement.

S&P 500 Stock Index Another thermometer for the overall health of the market, this index comprises the 500 largest public companies in the United States.

Securities and Exchange Commission (SEC) The nation's stock exchanges, as well as investment professionals, are watched over by this federal agency.

SIMPLE IRA An acronym, actually: Savings Incentives Match Plan for Employees IRA. This is set up by your employer, and companies with more than 100 employees can't offer these.

Solo 401(k) An option if you are self-employed and don't have any full-time employees. A nice feature of the solo 401(k) is the generous contribution limits.

Spousal IRA If you are a stay-at-home spouse who doesn't work, this account allows you to get around the requirement that you must have an earned income to contribute to an IRA. It can be a great way to double up on the amount you and your spouse are contributing to your retirement.

Step-Up This is a capital gains tax term. Whenever an asset is transferred from a deceased's ownership to his or her heir, rather than having to pay tax on the appreciation of the asset, the *cost basis* is reset to the value at the time of death, or 9 months later, whichever is higher.

Structured Settlement Could be part of a financial or insurance agreement. Structured settlement owners receive periodic payments over time in accordance with the terms of the agreement.

Substantially Equal Periodic Payments (SEPP) You are worrying about this if, for whatever reason, you find it necessary to withdraw money from your retirement account. There is ordinarily a 10% tax penalty, in addition to regular taxes, on amounts withdrawn. However, under a SEPP agreement, the 10% penalty can be waived. There are serious considerations about this option, and obviously, withdrawing from your retirement account should be your absolute last resort, but in emergencies a SEPP can be a good way to save you from getting dinged.

Systematic Withdrawal Plan (SWP) This is your blueprint for generating income in retirement. Take it seriously: set it out in as much detail as possible, and stick to it.

Target-Date Fund This is a type of mutual fund that is automatically balanced and rebalanced to reflect an investors needs, according to a predetermined *glide path*. If the approach sounds cookie-cutter, that's because it is. There is an appropriate application of these, but in the main, there's nothing magical about them, and above all, remember that returns aren't guaranteed.

Tax Basis Another term for *Cost Basis (above)*.

Tax-Deferred (Tax-Sheltered) Income that you put in various retirement accounts is often tax-deferred, meaning you'll only have to pay taxes on the amounts as they are withdrawn.

Thrift Savings Plan This is a DC savings plan for federal employees and uniformed services.

Trustee-to-Trustee Transfer When assets are moved from one account of the same type to another with no need to report it, meaning the move is tax-free.

Value Stock This is an investment that offers slower and steadier growth, and with that, more security. The company that offers this stock likely appears sound, and its actual worth is potentially more than its price suggests.

Variable Annuity This is an insurance product that, after the *accumulation stage*, pays income payments that vary depending on the performance of the markets the money is invested in.

Vesting This gives an employee rights to employer-provided assets over time. As an employee, you'll accrue ownership (which in non-forfeitable). The idea is that this incentivizes employees to perform well and stay with the company.

INDEX

SID MIRAMONTES

For the past 20 years, Sid has received various awards and recognitions for his achievements as a financial advisor. Sid began his career working at major wire houses, becoming Senior Vice President and Managing Director- Wealth Management before founding Miramontes Capital in 2015. Since 1995, Sid has helped to plan and manage more than a thousand individuals throughout their lives.

NOTES ON SOURCES

1   "Fiduciary Responsibilities." Department of Labor. dol.gov. *Web.* 20 Feb 2016.

2   "Putting Too Much Stock in Your Company—A 401(k) Problem." *Finra.org.* Financial Industry Regulatory Authority, Inc. 9 Sept. 2007. Web. 20 May 2015.

3   Rhee, Nari and Ilana Boivie: "The Continuing Retirement Savings Crisis," *nirsonline.org.* National Institute on Retirement Security. March 2015. Web. 18 May 2015.

4   Schrass, Daniel, Sarah Holden, and Michael Bogdan. 2015. "American Views on Defined Contribution Plan Saving." ICI Research Report. Washington, DC: Investment Company Institute (January).

5   "How Much Care Will You Need?" longtermcare.gov. *U.S. Department of Health and Human Services.* Web. 22 December, 2015.

6   As of April, 2015.
"Research, Statistics, and Policy Analysis—Monthly Statistical Snapshot." *Ssa.gov.* Social Security Administration. April 2015. Web. 15 April 2015.

7   "After the Storm: Three Unique Generations with Very Different Retirements Ahead of Them." *Transamericacenter.org.* Transamerica Center for Retirement Studies. 30 April 2014. Web. 10 August 2015.

8   "Retirement Planner: Benefits By Year Of Birth." *ssa.gov.* Social Security Administration. Web. 9 August 2015.

9   Bell, Claes. "Did You Miss The Stock Market Rally? You're Not Alone." *Bankrate. com.* Bankrate, Inc. 9 April 2015. Web. 11 May 2015.

10   Learn more about the DALBAR's QAIB Here: http://www.qaib.com/

11   "Retirement Topics - Exceptions to Tax on Early Distributions." *Irs.gov.* Internal Revenue Service. 1 Sept. 2015. Web. 25 Sept. 2015.

12   Find more about state coincident indexes here, at the Federal Reserve Bank of Philadelphia. https://www.philadelphiafed.org/research-and-data/regional-economy/indexes/coincident/

A free eBook edition is available with the purchase of this book.

To claim your free eBook edition:

1. Download the Shelfie app.
2. Write your name in upper case in the box.
3. Use the Shelfie app to submit a photo.
4. Download your eBook to any device.

Shelfie

A **free** eBook edition is available
with the purchase of this print book.

CLEARLY PRINT YOUR NAME ABOVE IN UPPER CASE

Instructions to claim your free eBook edition:
1. Download the Shelfie app for Android or iOS
2. Write your name in **UPPER CASE** above
3. Use the Shelfie app to submit a photo
4. Download your eBook to any device

Print & Digital Together Forever.

Snap a photo

Free eBook

Read anywhere

The Morgan James
Speakers Group

www.TheMorganJamesSpeakersGroup.com

We connect Morgan James published
authors with live and online events
and audiences whom will benefit
from their expertise.

Printed in the USA
CPSIA information can be obtained
at www.ICGtesting.com
JSHW022344140824
68134JS00019B/1678

9 781683 501268